10·8
H

Local Government Briefings

The Politics of Local Socialism

Local Government Briefings

The Politics
of Local Socialism

JOHN GYFORD

University College London

London
GEORGE ALLEN & UNWIN
Boston   Sydney

George Allen & Unwin (Publishers) Ltd,
40 Museum Street, London WC1A 1LU, UK

George Allen & Unwin (Publishers) Ltd,
Park Lane, Hemel Hempstead, Herts HP2 4TE, UK

Allen & Unwin, Inc.,
Fifty Cross Street, Winchester, Mass 01890, USA

George Allen & Unwin Australia Pty Ltd,
8 Napier Street, North Sydney, NSW 2060, Australia

First published in 1985.

British Library Cataloguing in Publication Data

Gyford, John
  The politics of local socialism.–(Local government briefings; 3)
1. Labour Party (*Great Britain*) 2. Local officials and employees–England
3. Local government–England
I. Title.   II. Series
328.42′073   JS3185
ISBN 0-04-352213-0
ISBN 0-04-352214-9 Pbk

Library of Congress Cataloging in Publication Data

Gyford, John.
  The politics of local socialism.
(Local government briefings, 3)
Bibliography: p.
Includes index.
1. Socialism–Great Britain. 2. Local government–Great Britain.
3. Municipal government–Great Britain.
I. Title.
HX249.G94   335′.00941   85-6081
ISBN 0-04-352213-0 (U.S.: alk. paper)
ISBN 0-04-352214-9 (U.S.: pbk.: alk. paper)

Set in 10 on 11 point Times by Fotographics (Bedford) Ltd
and printed in Great Britain by Billing & Sons Ltd, London and Worcester

Contents

Preface

The emergence of radical Labour councils committed to exploring the socialist potential of local politics has excited much public comment and not a little media hysteria. The aim of this book is to provide a brief account of this phenomenon of local socialism and to offer some interpretations of, and speculations about, its significance and its prospects.

On close inspection local socialism proves to be a rather more variegated form of politics than is sometimes assumed: it also represents a series of initiatives which have largely developed from the bottom up rather than from the top down. Neither organizationally nor programmatically is there any one authoritative centre representing the totality of local socialism. This is perhaps only to be expected in view of the anti-centralist sentiments often expressed from within the local socialist camp. It remains to be seen however whether the absence of any such centre of direction or inspiration proves to be a weak point in local socialism's struggle against a Conservative government whose chosen route to a free market economy appears to lie through a strong central state. In the meantime the lack of any formal structure or canonical text means that local socialism cannot be conceived of as a single movement or as a single ideology but rather, as I shall suggest, as a syndrome of associated practices and ideas.

It is too early yet for a definitive study of the impact of these various practices and ideas on individual local communities, though the excellent set of essays edited by Martin Boddy and Colin Fudge (1984) has now marked out some of the territory that will need to be explored in that connection. In this book I am concerned with presenting a general overview of local socialism and with setting its emergence and some of its recent developments in a wider political context. The fact that local socialism has developed in a rather piecemeal fashion does not mean that it is unrelated to broader political trends. An understanding of its nature, and of its possible future, is therefore helped by relating it to recent changes and debates within both local government and socialism in Britain and sometimes elsewhere.

At certain points I have drawn on material which I have published in *New Society* (21 April 1983), *Local Government Studies* (January/February 1983 and July/August 1984) and *Labour*

Councillor (July 1984): I am grateful to the editors of those journals for their permission to reproduce the material concerned. I am also grateful to the then Social Science Research Council (now the Economic and Social Research Council) who provided a small grant for research at one stage in the book's preparation. My thanks also go to the various local government officers, councillors and political activists who have discussed their work with me in recent years: not all of those who agreed to be quoted would wish to be identified by name and I have therefore made personal anonymity the rule for occasional attributed remarks. Irene Morrish has once again earned my gratitude for her efficient typing of successive drafts.

Finally, let me offer a brief personal account of the mood in which I have approached the subject of this book. In the wake of Labour's election defeat in 1959 I suggested in a letter in *Tribune* that centralization and bureaucracy were political problems which the Labour Party ought not to ignore, and that a greater concern with issues such as local democracy was therefore called for. Since then my own twenty-five years' professional, political and academic experience of local government has reinforced that general view. In particular I find it hard to see how Labour can set its sights much beyond the range of the welfare state without facing up to the problems of what is meant by democratic practice in the context of socialism. To my mind local socialism opens up that question very clearly, albeit not always in ways intended by its advocates, and for that reason the debates within and around it have implications beyond the immediate confines of individual local authorities.

John Gyford

1 Municipal Socialism and After

[They] were public spenders. But they tended to be authoritarian: doing the right thing *for* people rather than with them. (David Blunkett, leader of Sheffield City Council; Blunkett, 1982, emphasis in original)

The agenda for the 1984 Labour Party conference contained thirty-two resolutions on local government. This was the largest number of resolutions on any single topic, even outnumbering that hardy perennial of Labour conferences, defence, which mustered only eighteen resolutions. At the conference itself delegates passed a resolution which not only condemned the attacks being made on local government spending by the Thatcher government but also declared the party's support for councils who felt forced to break the law in defiance of those attacks. The contents of the conference agenda indicated the extent to which local government had come to preoccupy Labour activists in the first half of the 1980s whilst the 'law-breaking' resolution indicated the wide degree of support or sympathy within the party for the strategies being advocated by certain left-wing Labour councils. From being at one time little more than something of a sideshow, and one largely neglected by the left of the party, local government had become a major focus of Labour's political activity, as a means both of generating opposition to the post-1979 Conservative government and of developing new ideas about the future of socialism.

Labour had of course been involved in local government ever since the party's earliest years. Indeed councillors from the Labour movement had taken control of West Ham briefly in 1898 and of Woolwich in 1903, before the party itself was created out of the Labour Representation Committee in 1906. Yet despite the party's early and continuing involvement in local government, the latter's place in its strategy gradually became subordinated to the requirements of the parliamentary road to socialism.

From municipal socialism to municipal labourism

When the Labour Party was created in 1906 it found itself the potential heir to a substantial legacy of ideas and practices collectively known as municipal socialism, whose origins lay in the previous century. Even as early as the 1830s two Radicals, Francis Place and J. A. Roebuck, had published a series of pamphlets on municipal reform in which they 'glimpsed a municipal future which might indeed lead to a form of local socialism' (Fraser, 1979, p. 19). However the more immediate and largely pragmatic forerunner of municipal socialism was the so-called 'gas-and-water socialism' pioneered in Birmingham by Joseph Chamberlain in the 1870s. Chamberlain justified his policies not only on the grounds of the public welfare but also by the argument that there were economies to be made through an efficient municipal management which could in turn produce profits with which to subsidize rate-borne expenditure. For socialists, notably, but not exclusively, those in the Fabian Society, it was however possible to give a more political emphasis to the potential of municipal socialism. It was the Fabians who were mainly responsible for encouraging the Independent Labour Party (ILP) of the late nineteenth century 'to capture municipal government with the aim of using it as an instrument for the achievement of some measure of constructive Socialism'. The ILP found the idea of municipal enterprise to be 'applicable to their immediate situation and yet wide and far-reaching enough in its Socialist objectives to make an idealistic appeal' (Cole, 1948, p. 289).

The original *Fabian Essays* in 1889, in addition to echoing Chamberlain's aspirations about making considerable profits out of municipal trading, also spoke of the importance of local authorities providing jobs for the unemployed. The beneficial role of local councils as employers became a major element in the policies of early Labour councillors who saw municipal trading as a means of securing the payment of trade union wage rates, limitations on the length of the working week and 'fair-contract' terms with private suppliers and contractors.

As well as seeing in municipal socialism a source of financial profit for the municipality and of better conditions for the workforce there were some who also saw in it a potential for greater democracy. Thus Sidney Webb (1910, p. 734) saw municipal socialism as a form of 'democratic organisation on the basis of the association of consumers for the supply of their own needs'. Such socialism could avoid the twin perils of uniformity and of statism and thus ensure that socialism was enriched both by variety and by greater local accountability. Yet Webb was also very conscious of the need to maximize efficiency and in this he was supported by the warning of H. G. Wells (1959, p. 209) that those who would municipalize must also 'develop the most efficient public bodies possible'. As the twentieth century progressed efficiency tended increasingly to become equated with economies of scale and by 1945 the public corporation had come to replace the local authority as Labour's main means for achieving common ownership of services and industry.

The retreat from municipal socialism was not however merely a consequence of succumbing to the apparent logic of economies of scale. It was also a consequence of the evolution of the Labour Party in the years between the two world wars. So long as Labour was a small third party in Parliament it was natural for many socialists to see local government as a more fruitful field of activity, and pioneering Labour councils such as Bradford used their powers to promote socialism as best they could at the local level. But with the emergence of Labour as a major parliamentary party in the 1920s the focus began to shift away from the town halls to Westminster. Parliamentary socialism came to be the dominant strategy with its notion that the road to socialism lay through the electoral capture of central government, followed by a planned reconstruction of society.

Drucker (1979, p. 68) has argued that 'Labour's commitment to planning is a consequence of its commitment to parliamentary politics'. Certainly from the 1930s through to the 1970s Labour accorded primacy to parliamentary politics and whatever the party's internal disputes over more or less nationalization virtually all sections of the party agreed that socialism involved central planning of some sort. Clearly if Parliament was indeed the main power centre in the land, and if socialism could be constructed from within it, then some form of national planning appeared a logical mechanism to employ. The consequences of this for local government however were to relegate it at best to a role of minor importance and at worst, if in the wrong political hands, to a potential source of obstruction to the plans of a socialist government. Accordingly in a 1930s pamphlet, *Local Government and the Socialist Plan*, Clement Attlee pointed out that a socialist government might need to employ commissioners who would be 'sent down into a locality to see that the will of the central government is obeyed and its plans implemented' (Attlee, n.d., p. 5).

The view of local government as in some sense the handmaiden of central government persisted in the decades after 1945, as the Labour Party established itself as a major party of government. Labour came to see the major potential of local authorities to lie in their role in translating the aims of socialist legislation into reality on the ground. Where they were thought incapable of this their powers might be transferred to other specially created bodies, as in the case of the National Health Service and the gas and electricity industries. Labour representatives in local government were not universally happy as the emphasis shifted from municipalization to nationalization with its implicit downgrading of the role of local government.

The dissenting view was clearly expressed by a former Labour Lord Mayor of Manchester, Wright Robinson:

> With the advent of a Labour Government, and an unexampled volume of legislation, Local Government is definitely ending one important chapter of its history and beginning another. Municipalisation of so-called trading and other services has been one of the main planks in Labour's platform. Many of these services are now in the process of being transferred from municipal management and control to that of centralised or regional control ... What the thousands of Labour representatives in Local Government desire to know is how far local interest and participation in local affairs are to be retained ... The trend towards centralisation was not initiated by the present Government but by reason of the accelerated pace and increasing volume of legislation it has turned what was a drift into a drive towards centralisation. Many socialists in Local Government feel that a point has been reached in this drive when technical efficiency is being pursued without sufficient consideration being given to the long term effect on the democratic efficiency of a human society. (Robinson, 1948, pp. 182 and 188)

However, despite a modest rearguard defence of local government in Cabinet by Herbert Morrison, notably on the question of the health service, municipalist views such as those of Wright Robinson proved ineffective. As the handmaidens of parliamentary socialism Labour local authorities would have a necessary but circumscribed role to play. The nature of that limited role came to be characterized by a primary concern for the bread and butter welfare issues which most affected Labour's traditional political constituency amongst the working class.

A major influence on the performance of that role was the style of local politics which Herbert Morrison had evolved during his years at Hackney and then at the London County County (LCC). One particular feature of the Morrisonian style was a belief that Labour councillors should hold themselves at some distance both from the local party and from the council's officers. On relations with the local Labour Party outside the council Morrison was clear that its influence should stop well short of instructing Labour councillors how to act. He warned the 1930 party conference that local government could not be operated 'on the basis of Councils being marionettes whose actions ought to be decided in detail from outside'. His approach was thereafter enshrined in the *Model Standing Orders for Labour Groups*. As for the matter of relations with officers, right from his early days as Mayor of Hackney in 1920 he had, unlike George Lansbury in Poplar, abhorred the notion that officers might be appointed on the basis of political sympathy for a Labour programme, claiming that it would encourage servility and toadyism. But he went further. As well as eschewing political sympathy he urged that councillors should forgo any social intimacy with officers: they should meet only in the course of local authority business and then only on formal terms.

Yet Morrison's desire for an arm's length relationship with council officers did not mean that he discounted their contribution. Far from it, for as his biographers have observed, 'Morrison always trusted the professional' (Donoughue and Jones, 1973, pp. 209–10). A combination of Labour politicians, committed to an active role for the public sector, and professional officers, eager to demonstrate their expertise in practical terms, was to prove a powerful coalition not only in the case of the LCC but elsewhere. As Labour secured control of a growing number of councils, especially after 1945, when universal suffrage for local elections was finally achieved, a recognizable pattern of activity emerged which, if not quite as ambitious as municipal socialism, could perhaps be described as municipal labourism.

By the late 1930s it was already clear that Labour-controlled councils were providing more generous public assistance benefits, more extensive maternity and child welfare services and more spending per child on education. In the decades after 1945 Labour control became widely associated with higher standards of service provision and more generous spending, especially in the case of redistributive and ameliorative services such as education, housing and welfare. Labour was more likely to submit plans for comprehensive secondary education, to build more council houses and to pay higher rate subsidies on housing (McHenry, 1938; Boaden, 1971; Sharpe and Newton, 1984). This municipal labourism was clearly well in tune with the then prevailing mood of the Labour Party and represented local government's contribution to the development of the post-1945 welfare state. Much of it took place within the framework of parliamentary legislation, or sometimes in response to ministerial exhortation, and it was greatly facilitated by the postwar economic boom which ensured resources for what might otherwise have been competing local priorities.

It should not be supposed that municipal labourism was promoted solely or even mainly through the direct and specific initiatives of local Labour politicians. In many cases the expansion of existing services or the initiation of new policies originated largely with local authority officers responding to what they saw as the broad predilections of Labour members. Identifying and working up new policy proposals were tasks for which many Labour groups had neither the time nor the resources: what they could do, and did, was to provide the political climate within which expansion and initiative could flourish. There were of course instances where bold Labour leadership provided a particularly vigorous input, with politicians and professionals working in something approaching a genuine active partnership. Harry Mason and George Hodgkinson provided examples in the context of the postwar replanning of Plymouth and Coventry respectively. Their work was often held out as a model for others to follow and in later years Michael Foot was to describe Mason's Plymouth as 'democratic Socialism in action' (Foot, 1984, p. 115). Yet policy-oriented leadership such as Mason and Hodgkinson provided seems to have been the exception rather than the rule. More common was the situation noted by Green (1981) in Newcastle in the early 1970s where senior members of the Labour group played no significant part in initiating policy decisions.

Problems of municipal labourism

However, Newcastle in the early 1970s, as described by Green, was clearly a different place from Newcastle in the early 1960s, for in the latter instance it had certainly been provided with a policy-oriented Labour leadership in the person of T. Dan Smith. The circumstances and the events of Smith's leadership provide an important insight into the distortions and perversions to which municipal labourism could occasionally fall victim and which sometimes overshadowed its more positive features.

Smith himself has been described as one of the 'men of the sixties, entrepreneurial figures who helped to fashion a new Britain of concrete town centres and tower blocks [and] industrialised housing' (Fitzwalter and Taylor, 1981, p. 6). By his own reckoning he was a man with a 'vision of a city' which would be 'the city of the future' (Smith, 1970, pp. 47 and 58). In his own way he reflected the enthusiasm for planned modernization and technological revolution which caught up both the Labour Party and, it seemed, the country at large in the run up to Harold Wilson's election victories of 1964 and 1966.

The notion of comprehensive redevelopment of town centres had had its origins in attempts to deal with widespread war damage and cities such as Coventry and Plymouth were often cited as examples of what it could achieve. However its appeal to those who instinctively saw planning as a 'good thing', whether for political or professional reasons, ensured its retention beyond the postwar years and by 1962 some 345 towns in England and Wales had their own schemes for comprehensive redevelopment. Similarly, high-rise housing had been seen during the war as a possible component of postwar reconstruction. Thus Ritchie Calder (1941, p. 51) urged that as well as building garden cities, 'let us gather up the endless "ways" and "crescents" and "groves", now spread out like patience cards, and stack them'. In the immediate postwar years this advice was not followed, with most local authority dwellings taking the form of houses. However, government changes in the housing subsidy system in 1956, government pressure towards adoption of industrialized building methods, and vigorous marketing by contractors produced a boom in high-rise housing from the late 1950s into the late 1960s.

There can be few who would claim that this particular period of urban redevelopment was one of unqualified success. The demolition of the high-rise blocks of that era which have since proved uninhabitable has now become almost commonplace. More generally the process of comprehensive redevelopment, whether for housing or for town centre schemes, all too often became associated with the enforced and resented destruction of familiar places and of established local patterns of employment, recreation, friendship and neighbourliness. The drastic changes which occurred in urban areas often bore most heavily on the least well off, living in areas where low land and property values offered the prospect of major financial gain, to both public and private sectors, after redevelopment. In many areas grass-roots community groups emerged which tried to prevent, or to deflect elsewhere, the advent of the bulldozer: although they were to prove the origins of a widespread community action movement their immediate attempts to defend their own neighbourhoods often ended in failure. For some of those involved the bitterest irony was when they realized that the council whose plans they were contesting was controlled by the Labour Party to whom they would normally have expected to look for protection of their interests.

Apart from being implicated in some of the housing and planning disasters of the 1960s municipal labourism was also touched by various corruption scandals which accompanied the redevelopment boom. Here again T. Dan Smith provides the symbolic figure, since he was eventually, in 1974, to be sentenced to six years imprisonment on charges of corruption and conspiracy to corrupt: during the 1960s he had received £155,000 from the architect John Poulson for whom he had secured work which he, Smith, estimated to be worth £50 million. Smith was not alone: a modest procession of Labour local government figures made their way through the courts during the corruption trials of the early 1970s. Those convicted included Labour councillors whose former positions had been those of Leader of Wandsworth Council, Leader and Lord Mayor of Bradford, Leader and Chairman of Mexborough Council, Lord Mayor of Newcastle, Chairman of Chester-le-Street Rural District Council, Chairman of Durham County Planning Committee, Mayor of Pontefract, Leader and Chairman of Durham County Council, Leader and Chairman of

Durham County Council and Leader of Felling Urban District Council, Leader of Swansea Council, Leader of Port Talbot Council, Chairman of Port Talbot Housing Committee and Chairman of Rhondda Planning Committee.

The revelations during these trials were such as to cause the Labour Party to establish a special committee to inquire into the party's conduct in local government. The committee's report, published in June 1975, in addition to making specific recommendations about the organization and conduct of Labour groups, exhorted Labour councillors to avoid untoward pressures 'by keeping procedures as open as possible and by the most vigorous political campaigning to keep important local issues before the public'. This particular exhortation touched on some of the major weaknesses which had sometimes afflicted municipal labourism. These weaknesses helped to explain how a form of local politics which could often be imaginative and caring could also on occasions stumble into the errors of insensitive planning and high-rise housing and into the quagmire of public sector corruption – a crime which Herbert Morrison himself had regarded as the only one truly deserving capital punishment.

Of course the follies and venalities of housing and planning in the 1960s cannot all be laid at the doors of Labour councillors: others were also involved. Nevertheless the particular concentration of some of the corruption cases in such Labour heartlands as parts of Yorkshire, the North-East and South Wales highlighted a problem which was not wholly confined to those areas. An analysis of local authority proceedings in the 1960s had shown that the existence of a Labour majority was associated with short council meetings, few questions, few items referred back for reconsideration, low attendance of the public, less ready availability of council documents to the press, and restricted admission of the public to committee meetings (Boaden, 1971, pp. 112–14). In any event the key decisions were likely to be taken in private meetings of the ruling Labour groups and thereafter maintained by a strong system of party discipline. Such a system was not without its problems. After Labour's general election defeat in 1959 the party's National Executive Committee (NEC) concluded that 'the activities of certain local Labour groups . . . did detract from the image of the party' and the general secretary, Morgan Phillips, complained about Labour councils restricting the rights of the press and of council tenants (NEC Minutes, 28 October 1959); at the party conference soon afterwards the leader, Hugh Gaitskell criticized the 'apparently arbitrary and intolerant behaviour' of some Labour authorities. Much of the concern at this time was couched in terms of the adverse publicity such conduct might bring. Yet the problem in these cases was more than one of image or publicity.

The real problem was that in an attempt to maintain discipline and solidarity in what was seen as a potentially hostile world Labour groups and the councils they controlled had sometimes become not merely secretive but also increasingly remote from those whom they sought to serve. Far from being 'open' and 'campaigning' as the 1975 report was to recommend they had on occasions been closed and inward looking. In predominantly working-class areas, where Labour was deeply entrenched, there could easily emerge, as Dunleavy found in Newham, the 'closed and strong authority, virtually never affected by genuine electoral competition, dominating and controlling an extremely weak interest-group process and run for very long stretches of time by the small group of council leaders . . . [and in which] the constituency Labour parties were extensively manned by councillors' (Dunleavy, 1981, p. 335). Some of the attitudes of such authorities might well be found even in the case of Labour councils who were less 'closed' or 'strong'. For example, when Arthur Skeffington presented his report on *Public Participation in Planning* at the 1970 Labour local government conference the air was filled with cries of scorn and disagreement from a variety of Labour councillors who all insisted that they were perfectly well in touch with the people and that more widespread 'public participation' was merely a trojan horse for the middle classes. As for relations with the press, most Labour councillors regarded it as endemically anti-Labour and not really worth cultivating. Press reports of corruption in Labour authorities could thus be, and were, dismissed as the work of the capitalist media determined to hound socialist politicians.

The problems of closed and strong Labour councils did not stop with the problems of their relations with their local communities: there was also the problem of their attitude towards policy-making. Members of the more securely entrenched Labour groups were drawn largely from the ranks of manual workers and the more modest white collar workers such as school teachers, insurance agents and trade union officials. As local government officers increasingly became, in the 1950s and 1960s, a body of graduate-entry professionals there began to open up an educational and cultural gap between them and many of the councillors they served. Policy-making became, or appeared to become, an increasingly complex and esoteric activity: one result was that 'members' grasp on their authority's policies was quite vague, even if they had been chairman or vice-chairman at some stage' (Dunleavy, 1981, p. 341). Labour members were often very assiduous at case-work. Some of them derived a certain satisfaction from civic pomp and circumstance and from the fruits of patronage politics in the form of committee chairmanships and nominations to other public bodies; but for unpaid part-time amateurs the details of policy-making could be too much to hope to master, thus leaving a vacuum into which others could and did step. The closed and strong Labour authority, with councillors who were both quiescent and acquiescent, was a body ripe for instruction and leadership, whether from an outstanding councillor, a dynamic professional officer, a proselytizing Whitehall department or a developer with an eye to the main chance. As such it was a hostage to fortune, capable of being employed for ends that might be good or bad or a mixture of the two.

The purpose of rehearsing some of the problems of municipal labourism is not to denigrate its often considerable achievements in the field of human welfare. For all its faults municipal labourism, like the postwar welfare state of which it formed a part, secured considerable real improvements in the material conditions of working-class life. On occasion however it was prone to two weaknesses. It could display a certain heavy-handed paternalism, leading to an insensitivity to the self-expressed interests of ordinary people when these seemed to conflict with the plans or the enthusiasms of senior councillors or of professionals and other experts; and a certain introverted emphasis on political solidarity and discipline could sometimes blind local councillors to legitimate outside criticism or could even be exploited for dubious ends. At its best municipal labourism matched Herbert Morrison's aspiration to create in local government 'an efficient machine for a high moral purpose' and it delivered with competence and compassion a wide range of services to those in need. Usually it did the right things *for* people; but sometimes it could do the wrong things *to* people; and only rarely had it previously discussed either of those things *with* people.

Poplarism and the left

There were occasional instances where Labour councils were unwilling to stay within the confines of conventional municipal labourism, particularly where their own interpretations of local need conflicted with those laid down by Parliament or government. This phenomenon of the 'rebel' council took an early and dramatic shape in the 1920s in the case of Poplar where Labour controlled both the borough council and the board of guardians who administered the Poor Law. In a protest against the government's failure to equalize the rate burden as between rich and poor areas of London the council refused in 1921 to levy the precepts of the LCC, the Metropolitan Police and the Metropolitan Asylums Board. Thirty councillors were sent to prison where they remained for six weeks before being released; but legislation was soon passed which secured a pooling of the cost of outdoor poor relief in London. The Poplar guardians meanwhile continued in dispute with the government over their payment of poor relief at levels higher than the latter approved. In 1922 the Minister of Health issued an Order prohibiting payment of relief in excess of the approved scale and imposing surcharges on the guardians for payments over the limit. The payments continued however and no attempt was made to apply the Order or to collect the surcharge.

In 1929, with the abolition of the Poor Law, all boards of guardians were replaced by local authority public assistance committees and as the depression deepened a number of localities followed the example of Poplar in paying higher rates of assistance to the unemployed than the government wished. More than twenty authorities, not all of them Labour-controlled, mounted what one historian has described as the 'most widespread rebellion by local government in the twentieth century' (Stevenson, 1984, p. 310) by refusing to operate the means test as rigorously as the government required. One by one however the authorities drew back from outright confrontation until only Labour-controlled Rotherham and Durham County Council were left: in October and November 1932 these last two had their public assistance committees superseded by commissioners appointed by the government. In 1934 Neville Chamberlain took the whole issue 'out' of local politics by transferring unemployment relief to a new Unemployment Assistance Board.

To Conservatives the term 'Poplarism' came to signify the defiance of central government by (usually Labour) local authorities in the name of the right to overspend. To the Labour politicians involved, the crucial question was not really one of the financial relations between central and local government. Poplar's Mayor, George Lansbury, saw matters thus:

The issue that is raised by Poplar is larger than an issue of local government ... It is the whole question of whether the Labour movement means business. Are we going to attempt to carry out what we say on the platform, or are we to be misled and side-tracked by considerations of 'statesmanship'? (Quoted in Branson, 1979, p. 165)

Poplarism and its disdain for 'statesmanship' did not find favour with Herbert Morrison. For one thing he feared that defiance of a Conservative government by Labour councils opened the way for Conservative councils one day to defy a Labour government. More generally however he saw Poplarism as threatening Labour's chances of establishing itself as a reliable and competent party of government rather than as a provoker of chaos. None the less, despite the existence of such doubts within the party, there were to be other instances of left Labour councils insisting on ploughing their own furrow no matter how much it might displease or embarrass the party leadership. Moreover their justification of their own actions would echo the sort of sentiments expressed by Lansbury in defence of Poplar.

Thus in opposing the Housing Finance Act 1972 the council at Clay Cross 'saw itself as a socialist council trying to carry out socialist policies which had been upheld by the Party its members belonged to' (Skinner and Langdon, 1974, p. 90). When South Yorkshire ran into difficulties with a Labour government between 1975 and 1977 over bus fares policy its leader, Sir Ron Ironmonger, complained about the government 'pressurising councils like South Yorkshire to abandon their mandate from the Labour Party and the electorate' (*Sheffield Forward*, July 1976). A similar defence was mounted when Liverpool delayed its rate-making in 1984 in an attempt, only partially successful, to wrest financial concessions from the government:

> The policies we have campaigned for on the council are solidly backed by Liverpool District Labour Party, by local trades unionists, and by those who voted Labour last May. Why? Because they recognise that socialist policies are the only way to defend workers' interests. (Militant, 1984, p. 2)

The recurrent theme in such defences of Poplar and its latter day descendants was thus the existence of a popular local mandate for. genuinely socialist policies which claimed priority over any other considerations urged by party leaders or by the government of the day. Such an argument was based, implicitly if not explicitly, on a belief that local government should be conducted within a framework of ideological politics in which 'unified political parties provide specific programmes' (Hill, 1972, p. 211) which the politicians implement once elected. Given its head maybe the municipal socialism of the pre-1918 era would have taken on the character of just such an ideological politics: certainly the vigorous public debates on the merits or otherwise of municipal trading during the early years of the century lent themselves to that sort of politics. However the shift of the main emphasis of Labour's challenge to the parliamentary level after 1918 somehow defused much of the ideological contest at the local level. Thereafter municipal labourism had leant not towards ideological politics but rather towards an administrative politics (Hill, 1972) in which councillors placed reliance on the practical abilities of their professional officers rather than on their own ideological zeal in order to serve the interests of their communities. Under this form of politics the officers consulted the politicians and constructed policies which they thought would satisfy them, or at least not offend them. Rarely though would the politicians arrive in the council chamber with clearly articulated policies in the form of a detailed manifesto. Thus it was that Labour's general secretary could complain to the party's local government conference in 1960: 'One of the biggest faults I see in local election material is its vagueness – it is so platitudinous, it doesn't say anything'.

Within such a conception of administrative local politics acts of ideological defiance such as those of Poplar and its successors might well seem brave, or foolhardy, acts of socialist virtue but they ran counter to the prevailing ethos. Rather than work against the grain most Labour councils were likely to adopt an attitude similar to that expressed by West Ham in 1932 when they declined to follow Rotherham and Durham into last-ditch defiance over the means test: 'we prefer to keep our poor under our own care and do what we can for them rather than hand them over to an arbitrary Commissioner from whom they could expect little humanity' (quoted in Branson and Heinemann, 1971, p. 28). It was better to give what little practical help one could rather than to die in the last ideological ditch.

For many on the left of the Labour Party the administrative politics of municipal labourism was not to their taste: it had a 'fusty, Fabian reformist image' (Leeson, 1981, p. 18). The left concentrated their main energies on national issues such as public ownership, foreign policy and defence and on problems such as the relations between party conference and the parliamentary leadership. The nature and ambitions of parliamentary socialism were their primary concerns. They understood the frustrations of one of their then heroes, Aneurin Bevan, who after election to Tredegar Urban District Council in 1922, found that 'the power *had* been there but it had just gone . . . to the County Council' (his emphasis); so he secured election to the County Council in 1928 but 'I got there and it had gone from there too'. As Bevan's biographer says, within such local authorities 'much good administrative work was accomplished'; but for a left-winger that was not enough and battle had to be joined with 'the edicts of the Government at Westminster and the economic system it sustained'. Only at Westminster would Bevan be able to lay hold of the power to change things: meanwhile he feared 'Some of those Councils stewed in their own juice so long they became rancid' (Foot, 1975, pp. 86–7). For socialists it was right to 'assert the wisdom of collective action through Parliament as the core of their creed' (Bevan, 1952, p. 32). In recent times, however, that wisdom has come to be challenged as some on the left have argued the merits of extra-, though not necessarily anti-, parliamentary politics within which local government might have a significant part to play.

Local socialism and the new urban left

The Left is now in control of many Boroughs . . . The leadership of London is now ours.

So more wolves leap out of sheep's clothing.

It was with these contrasting reactions that *London Labour Briefing* (June 1982) and the *Daily Telegraph* (2 June 1982) respectively greeted the emergence of left-wing Labour leaderships in the wake of the 1982 local elections in Camden, Greenwich, Hackney, Haringey, Islington and Southwark. Despite their very different responses the two journals were agreed in recognizing the significance of a new phenomenon, namely the emergence of the Labour left as a powerful force in urban government in the capital. The six boroughs were not unique as scenes of a left victory, for in the previous year the Greater London Council (GLC), the Inner London Education Authority (ILEA) and Merseyside County Council has also come under the control of the left. Paradoxically, the 1982 local elections had seen the defeat of existing left administrations in Walsall and, temporarily, in Lambeth. Further north Sheffield and South Yorkshire had already provided pioneering examples of what a left Labour council might try to achieve, whilst Stirling was acquiring a similar reputation in Scotland.

The 1982 elections were subsequently shown not to be a temporary aberration. The left gained control of Liverpool in 1983 as Labour displaced the Liberals and of Manchester in 1984 as the left displaced the right in the controlling Labour group.

The Labour left's involvement in local government thus showed clear signs of extending beyond its historic occasional concern with embattled councils like those of Poplar or Clay Cross. Nor was it now confined solely to those local authorities on which the Labour left were in control of the ruling majority group. A *Sunday Times*/MORI survey of six English local authorities, carried out in the summer of 1982, found that 44 per cent of Labour councillors identified themselves as being on the left of the party, with a further 24 per cent calling themselves left of centre: a mere 5 per cent admitted to being on the right or right of centre (Lipsey, 1982).

To talk of left Labour councils and councillors is to use a form of political shorthand, for historically 'the Labour Left has been a loose association of individuals and tendencies, often shifting its composition from issue to issue' (Pimlott, 1980, p. 163). Thus the older *Tribune* left has in recent years been outflanked by a newer left which has talked, not always in unison, in a more consistently Marxist language. However even allowing for problems in con-

structing a watertight definition of the Labour left it is clear that it
grew in strength throughout the 1970s and into the 1980s, its relative
strength within the party being particularly enhanced by right-wing
defections to the Social Democratic Party (SDP) in 1981. The new
elements of the left embraced a variety of groups and factions. They
differed on certain points, whether of substance or of emphasis, but
the general thrust of their strategy was in the direction outlined in
1980 by Peter Hain of the Labour Co-ordinating Committee, itself
one of the new left-wing groups. He observed that the 'new Labour
left', as he described it, rejected the 'insurrectionary' approach of the
far left, such as the Socialist Workers' Party (SWP), the International
Marxist Group and the Workers' Revolutionary Party. But it also
rejected the 'parliamentary' approach, which

> refused to concede that parliament is only one of a series of power
> bases and that, by comparison with others such as the business
> world, civil service, the police, armed forces, and the media, its
> power is heavily circumscribed and in any case subject to the
> dictates of capitalism.

Accordingly, the new Labour left was 'to be distinguished from the
tradition of Nye Bevan and Michael Foot'. Unlike them, the new
Labour left,

> while acknowledging the importance of gaining a parliamentary
> majority to legitimate and encourage the process of change, . . .
> recognises that this will fail unless a priority is given to extra-
> parliamentary struggle and campaigning . . . With that in mind the
> [new] Labour left is seeking to build alliances with rank and file
> trade unionists, with community groups, the women's movement,
> and with single-issue or protest campaigns, so that they can help to
> give new impetus to the Labour movement, ultimately trans-
> forming it. (Hain, 1980c, pp. 13–14)

Hain's characterization of the new Labour left accords well with
the exhortation which appeared in *London Labour Briefing* in June
1982 heralding a meeting to set up an Association of Socialist
Councillors:

> Labour Councillors need to break out of the confines of Council
> Chamber politics and link up with those 'extra-parliamentary
> forces' – the trade unions, ethnic minority organisations, women's
> movement, tenants' and residents' organisations, etc., etc., – which
> alone can provide the forces for a real fight.

It is, of course, arguable that there is nothing especially 'new' in
such an approach. Back in 1968, for example, the *May Day*

Manifesto of Stuart Hall, Raymond Williams and E. P. Thompson
had spoken of the need to

> stop subordinating every issue, and every strategy, to electoral
> calculations and organizations . . . To be a socialist now is . . . to be
> where a school or a hospital needs urgent improvement, or where a
> bus-service, a housing development, a local clinic needs to be
> fought through against the ordinary commercial and bureaucratic
> priorities. (Hall *et al.*, 1969, pp. 140–1)

Yet the new left which had existed in the late 1960s, in the years of
student unrest and anti-Vietnam protest, directed much of its energy
into teach-ins, campus revolts, anti-war demonstrations and the
counter-culture; at the local level it concerned itself with
community-based action against local authorities rather than with
involvement in the party politics of local government. One of the
distinctive features of the contemporary new Labour left compared
with its predecessors has been not so much its enthusiasm for extra-
parliamentary politics but its readiness to see involvement in local
government as a worthwhile way in which to pursue that form of
politics.

Identifying the scale or extent of that involvement presents
something of a problem for there is no single criterion which can be
applied. If one attempts to use the adoption of particular policies
conventionally associated with the left as guides to the presence of the
left in local government then the situation does not necessarily
become crystal clear. For example about one hundred and fifty
councils have declared themselves nuclear-free zones or have
otherwise opposed the manufacture or deployment of nuclear
weapons within their boundaries. Yet the first steps in this direction
were taken by Manchester City Council when under right-wing
Labour control in 1980 and some of the other councils who followed
Manchester's example, such as Inverness, Cleethorpes and Wigtown,
were in non-Labour hands at the time.

A very much smaller number of authorities, twenty-two by late
1984, had set up working parties or full committees to promote the
interests of women, another issue associated with the left: they
included the GLC, nine London boroughs, the Merseyside and West
Midlands metropolitan counties, and major cities such as
Birmingham, Edinburgh, Leeds, Newcastle and Nottingham, some of
them, such as Birmingham and Newcastle, led by the Labour right. A
roughly similar number of authorities were also developing specific
initiatives on race relations. A conspicuous absentee from both lists is
Liverpool where women's issues, along with race issues, have been
seen as subordinate to class-based politics. Liverpool would also be

absent from any list of authorities committed to the decentralization of local services, a strategy pioneered on socialist grounds in 1980 by Walsall, taken up after 1982 by some London boroughs and adopted in 1984 by the right-wing led Labour group in Birmingham. On the other hand Liverpool would clearly figure on a list of councils opposed to the increasingly authoritarian local government policies of the Thatcher government: but then so would probably all Labour councils and quite a number of others as well. If, however, one tried to group local authorities by the nature of their preferred strategies of opposition then differences, even if only of style or of timing, could be found even between authorities generally regarded as firmly on the left such as Liverpool and Sheffield let alone between Liverpool and a more right-wing Labour authority such as Newcastle.

It is possible to conceive of left-wing local government in terms of left-wing councillors, left-wing local authorities and left-wing policies, but as we have seen the three sets of phenomena do not enjoy an identical overlap. There are for example some councillors, left-wing by their own and others' perceptions, who serve on authorities not controlled by the left; there are some self-avowedly left-wing authorities which do not embrace quite the same package of policies as do others; and there are some policies associated with the left which have proved to have an appeal extending beyond their own ranks. It is therefore impossible to present a neatly quantified three-dimensional definition of left-wing local government. Certain local authorities undoubtedly recur in any attempt to discuss the subject. They include the GLC, the ILEA, the Merseyside and South Yorkshire County Councils, several of the London boroughs, major cities such as Liverpool, Manchester and Sheffield, smaller authorities such as Stirling, or Walsall between 1980 and 1982. The number of such authorities however may yet be subject to the vagaries of electoral change and, in some cases, to abolition by Act of Parliament. As for the councillors and the policies one can perhaps talk of a 'new urban left' and of 'local socialism'.

The new urban left is not a formally organized grouping. One of its members has described it as almost amoeba-like in its lack of any one constant pattern of organization. It includes not only councillors but also party activists, community workers and local government officers (some of whom also serve as councillors on other local authorities). They share a common concern for the socialist potential of local government arising often from a belief in the inadequacy of traditional models of socialist politics. They seek a new local road to socialism free from what they regard as the centralized deformations of both the parliamentary and the insurrectionary roads: they are the local government wing of the extra-parliamentary new left. Their membership has ranged across, among others, the Labour

Co-ordinating Committee, the Socialist Campaign for Labour Victory, the Socialist Environment and Resources Association (SERA), and the Clause Four group: their writings have appeared in periodicals such as *Labour Activist, Socialist Organiser, Labour Herald, Local Socialism, Chartist, Marxism Today, New Socialist* and the various *Labour Briefing* journals such as those in London, Brighton, Manchester and Merseyside. They contribute to and draw upon a growing literature of booklets and pamphlets published by local community groups, the Labour Co-ordinating Committee, the Conference of Socialist Economists, the Institute for Workers' Control, SERA and Independent Labour Publications (heir to the old ILP).

This new urban left has a variety of specific origins. Among them are community action and community development; campaigns against local spending cuts; the internal struggles between left and right for control of local Labour parties; the radicalization of some of the local government professions; environmentalism; the women's movement; and even the former Hain-ite wing of the Young Liberals. Uniting them, albeit somewhat loosely on occasions, is a commitment to some form of locally based socialism as a worthwhile strategy for socialist advance.

The nature of this local socialism is best understood not in terms of a single coherent ideology but as a syndrome or a set of associated characteristics. These characteristics would include: a concern for issues hitherto absent from or marginal to conventional local government, such as local economic planning, monitoring the police, women's rights, and racial equality; a disdain for many of the traditional ways of conducting local authority business; a view of local government as an arena both for combating the policies of a Conservative government and for displaying by example the potential of a grass-roots socialism; and, perhaps most fundamentally, a commitment to notions of mass politics based upon strategies of decentralization and/or political mobilization at the local level.

As already indicated not all those in the new urban left would necessarily endorse all these elements of local socialism; similarly there are elements of local socialism which would be endorsed by those not normally seen, by themselves or others, as part of any new urban left. Between them nevertheless their emegence has represented an identifiably new departure both for British local government and for British socialism.

Much media space has been devoted to the new style of activity undertaken by left-wing authorities, especially in fields not hitherto seen by the media as being any business of local government – proclaiming nuclear-free zones, discussing Northern Ireland, funding radical community groups, flying red flags, setting up women's committees and race relations committees, appointing political sympathizers to key posts, encouraging municipal enterprise and workers' co-operatives and questioning the rights and duties of the police and the courts. The extent of the media coverage is indicated by the emergence of Ken Livingston, leader of the GLC, as second only to the pope in BBC Radio's Man of the Year poll in 1982; by 1984 Livingstone had also become the subject of a biography by a leading journalist (Carvel, 1984). However it would be wrong to assume from the extent of the coverage that it was necessarily favourable. In the London *Standard* (2 December 1982) Max Hastings saw leftist councillors as 'ugly, nasty, with power the only aim'; in *The Times* (11 January 1983) the Tory philosopher Roger Scruton saw them as 'vociferating infants striving for attention'; Islington in particular was singled out as 'Britain's barmiest council' (*Daily Telegraph*, 13 December 1982) and as the 'Town Hall Follies' (*Sunday Times*, 13 May 1984).

In terms of its relations with the press however the left did not always help matters. The GLC's attempt to procure an apology from the *Standard* for a JAK cartoon, thought to be offensive to the Irish, by withdrawing its advertising was described in a Press Council judgement in 1983 as 'a blatant attempt by a local authority to use the power of its purse to influence the contents of a newspaper and coerce the editor'. In the same year Islington's denial of information, assistance and advertising to the *Islington Gazette* in the context of a dispute between its publishers and the National Union of Journalists was seen by the Press Council as 'a deplorable example of councillors disregarding their responsibility not to impede the free flow of information'. The councillors' attempts to provide their own flow of information through a council-sponsored *Islington News* subsequently collapsed with heavy financial losses in 1984. The problem of securing accurate reporting of left-wing councils cannot however be attributed solely to the councils themselves as is seen in a Press Council judgement in 1984 relating to events in Brent where the left at the time narrowly held control. On this occasion the Press Council censured the *Daily Telegraph* for an article on education in Brent which it condemned as 'seriously inaccurate, confused and confusing and highly prejudicial' and 'based heavily on assertion and hearsay'.

In general the impression which was created by much of the media, especially perhaps by the press, was that the activities of the new urban left were quite beyond all possible reason, only explicable in terms of folly or wickedness or both. Such a view was not unlike that held by the Conservative government whose members sometimes explained the case for abolition of the GLC and the metropolitan counties partly in terms of the need to rid the country of such alleged strongholds of this new form of socialism. Yet the government's very attempt to rid the country of those selfsame local authorities was to prove far more laborious and far less popular than probably was foreseen; local socialism proved to be a wily opponent with some considerable tactical skills.

The nature of this local socialism, its origins and its aspirations, can in fact be considered in terms other than those of its sworn opponents or of the media. This is not to say that it should be taken wholly at its own self-evaluation. But it is to suggest that a reasonably cool examination might be able to identify both its strengths and its weaknesses and thus to contribute to some understanding of a phenomenon which involves a simultaneous reappraisal of certain received notions both about local government and about socialism.

2   The Emergence of Local Socialism

> The influx of people that have given the GLC this great reputation in the gutter press for being the end of civilisation as we know it, is the fact that it is the post-1968 generation in politics. (Ken Livingstone, leader of the GLC, interviewed in *Marxism Today*, November 1981)

Although local socialism was only discovered by the media in 1981 and 1982, albeit not under that name, its origins can be traced back well beyond those years. In terms of events in individual localities for example, the Greater London Labour Party executive was captured by the left in 1977; and two years previously a Labour Against the Cuts group had been set up by three left-wing GLC councillors, Tony Banks, Ken Livingstone and David White. In Liverpool a concerted effort to reconstruct the Labour Party on a left-wing basis, with *Militant* supporters heavily involved, began after the Liberals took control of the city council in 1974.

Important though such events in the mid-1970s may have been, the antecedents of local socialism can in fact be traced back even further, into the late 1960s. It was then that there began the series of changes and events in and around the Labour Party and its relations with local government which paved the way for the rise of the new urban left; and it was in the same period that there also emerged the first of a number of social movements and bodies of ideas which created a climate of opinion favourable to a more decentralized form of socialist politics in general and to local socialism in particular.

Changes and events

A changing party

In 1971 Barry Hindess published his book *The Decline of Working Class Politics*. Based on a study of Labour Party branches in Liverpool it argued that branches in working-class areas were proving less able to recruit and retain new active members than were branches in middle-class areas. Moreover this in turn was leading to a changing emphasis in the policy and political interests of the party in Liverpool as it became less and less oriented to local, specifically working-class, concerns and more to the ideological issues of national and international significance which preoccupied middle-class activists. This in turn made the party yet more unattractive to potential working-class activists.

Hindess's book created something of a controversy at the time and he himself has subsequently identified as a significant weakness its tendency towards sociological reductionism, namely 'the treatment of the working class as having interests that exist irrespective of whether members of the working class recognise them as such' (Hindess, 1983, p. 3). This particular approach, which 'is ubiquitous in left analyses of British politics' (ibid.), is one whose problems have some relevance to the nature of local socialism and we shall return to it later. For the moment however the particular importance of Hindess's book lies in the fact that it heralded a widespread and lasting concern over the scale and nature of Labour Party membership and activism.

Twelve years after Hindess's book, Whiteley (1983, p. 62) felt able to confirm 'that there has been a decline in working class activism in the Labour Party' and to add that 'this is one of the important reasons for the decline in party membership over time'. The stark evidence of declining party membership, leaving aside those who merely paid the political levy within their trade union, was very clear, even allowing for the crude nature of the returns sometimes submitted to headquarters by constituency parties. On the basis of the published figures Whiteley suggested that the party lost on average something like 11,000 members per year between 1949 and 1978 'and the true loss of membership may well be higher than this' (Whiteley, 1982, p. 111). In seeking a cause for this massive decline Whiteley placed particular stress on the failure of Labour governments, in the fields of economic and social policy, to satisfy the requirements of working-class members whose orientation to politics he saw as primarily instrumental rather than expressive, idealistic or ideological as in the case of their middle-class comrades. Working-class disillusion over these policy failures, plus a number of other factors, had produced a situation whereby Labour was being left with activists who were 'increasingly more middle-class, more ideological in their approach to politics and less concerned with pragmatic instrumental questions' (Whiteley, 1983, p. 79).

Individual surveys of different elements of the party certainly seemed to confirm the notion of a party whose activists were more and more drawn from the middle class, whether amongst MPs (Johnson, 1973), members of the NEC (Hanby, 1974), councillors (Gordon and Whiteley, 1979; Lipsey, 1982), or annual conference delegates (Whiteley, 1983). As well as reflecting a displacement of a disillusioned working-class membership this development may also have mirrored the dramatic growth in white-collar and professional employment in the United Kingdom after 1945. Much of this occurred in the public sector especially in local government, education and the health services. It was followed by an increasing membership, and later greater militancy, in some of the public sector and white-collar unions, with the 1970s seeing the first official nation-wide strikes called by the local government unions. In addition to such broad changes in the social structure there were also changes in the social geography of particular localities which had their impact on individual local Labour parties. For example, the process of 'gentrification' in parts of Inner London, involving the immigration into hitherto working-class areas of 'people who are not in business, but in teaching, architecture or similar professions' (Evans, 1973, pp. 11–12) seems to have had a very noticeable impact on the social and ideological complexion of local Labour parties (Baine, 1975; Glassberg, 1981). It is certainly apparent that in London it is the largely 'ungentrified' boroughs of Tower Hamlets, Newham and Barking and Dagenham which have thus far proved least fertile ground for the new urban left.

The social changes which the Labour Party has undergone in the recent past should not be seen as wholly peculiar to this country. During the same period, in the Australian Labour Party 'the professional element increased, while there was a relative decline in the traditional working-class element' (Duncan, 1983, p. 19); in New Zealand 'Labour Party members – particularly the active ones – are no longer predominantly blue-collar workers' (Vowles, 1983, p. 42; cf. Gustafson, 1976). In France the Socialist Party, which had never really been able to compete successfully with the Communist Party for working-class activists, was becoming by the early 1980s 'the Party of the tertiary (largely public) sector, credentialled (not propertied) middle class' (Bell and Criddle, 1984, p. 206). The other socialist and labour parties of Western Europe have also shown a tendency for 'the party membership to become more middle-class and for the number of working-class members to fall': this middle class however is not the private sector bourgeoisie but embraces instead 'the large new categories of peoples employed either by public authorities and in the "soft professions", and whose political attitudes may differ substantially from those of the more settled members of the middle-class and may, indeed, be more radical than those of most manual workers' (Paterson and Thomas, 1977, pp. 18–19).

The radicalization which the British Labour Party underwent as its social composition changed was also paralleled elsewhere. In the Dutch Labour Party a new left emerged in the late 1960s consisting 'of some individuals whose principal concerns were participatory democracy and greater well-being, some representatives of the youth culture, and a few neo-Marxists . . . many were involved in the "soft", newer service industries – universities, research institutes, the media, social work, private or governmental bureaucracies'. This new left gained in influence 'in part by being more active than other party members, in part by recruiting new members and in part by articulating the concerns felt by a [wider] portion of the party membership'. Its impact was such that

> earlier commitments to a more equal society have been fused with demands for greater participation and greater popular control at all levels . . . the Party became 'democratised' and power has become decentralised . . . Party sections suspiciously oversee the actions of municipal councillors and aldermen . . . At the same time the [party] is favourably disposed towards the various social action groups which have sprung up since the late 1960s. (Wolinetz, 1977, pp. 355, 361–2)

The Dutch experience in particular may serve to remind us that the British Labour Party is not quite so singular as its own insularity sometimes leads it to believe. However its own version of social change and radicalization did have a history of its own, which has been chronicled elsewhere (Hatfield, 1978; Kogan and Kogan, 1983). One particular feature of the British Labour Party's experience was that the growing influence of its left wing from the early 1970s onwards was accompanied by the persistence of major social problems in some major cities and by the emergence of a crisis in central–local government relations over the issue of local authority expenditure. Thus problems of local government began to intrude increasingly into the agenda of local Labour parties at the very time when the left was making its long march through the institutions and constitution of the party. Moreover since, unlike the insurrectionary left, it regarded such services as housing, education and social services as representing real gains for the working class, it felt bound to defend them against attack by local councils acting in compliance with the demands of central government. In some cases also left-wing party activists had begun to feel doubts about the socialist virtue of some existing Labour councillors and councils, doubts similar to those they already felt about Labour MPs and Labour governments. Perhaps most significantly of all however the left's ability to make an impact on local government was immeasurably enhanced by two particular sets of events, namely Labour's local election defeats in the late 1960s and local government reorganization in the early 1970s.

Electoral disaster

If any single set of events can be said to have eased the way for the eventual emergence of local socialism it was, paradoxically enough, the massive anti-government swings from Labour to the Conservatives in the local elections of 1967 and 1968.

In 1967 the Conservatives won control of the GLC and of ten county councils. They also took control of Bradford, Cardiff, Coventry, Leeds, Leicester, Liverpool, Manchester, Newcastle, Nottingham and Southampton. A total of over 1,500 seats passed from the Labour Party to the Conservatives in the elections to the GLC, the county councils and the provincial boroughs and urban districts. At that point it was Labour's worst set of local election results in any of the postwar years. Yet worse was to come in 1968.

In the London boroughs and in the provincial boroughs and urban districts in 1968 Labour secured less than 17 per cent of the seats: the Conservatives took 63 per cent. In the county boroughs Labour polled under 30 per cent: the Conservative share was 60 per cent. Overall Labour's net loss amounted to 1,602 seats: the Conservatives gained 1,630. The Conservatives had made substantial inroads into Labour strength in individual provincial towns and cities in 1967. Now further substantial gains were to be recorded – seven in Birmingham, eight in Dudley, twelve in Liverpool, eleven in Manchester, seven in Southampton, eight in Stoke-on-Trent. In Sheffield seven gains gave the Conservatives control for only the second time in forty-one years.

In Greater London the 1968 results were even more dramatic, for there all the councillors were up for re-election. Having gone into the elections controlling twenty of the London boroughs, Labour finished up controlling only four, Southwark, Tower Hamlets, Newham and Barking and of those, one, Newham, was retained only through use of the Labour mayor's casting vote. The size of the Conservative gains and Labour losses in individual boroughs was staggering. The Conservatives gained fifteen seats in Camden and in Croydon, twenty-one in Brent, thirty in Hackney, thirty-three in Haringey, thirty-five in Wandsworth, thirty-eight in Lambeth, forty-six in Hammersmith, forty-seven in Islington.

For the Conservatives such results were little short of a miracle: the new Conservative leader of Islington confessed to the *Evening Standard* (10 May 1968) that 'Never in my wildest dreams did I imagine that this would happen'. For his Labour opponents 'defeat at the polls came as a traumatic shock – eye-witnesses report that former Councillors broke down and cried' (Baine, 1975, p. 34). Quite apart from the sudden shock of defeat and loss experienced by individual councillors the results had another, more far-reaching, consequence. The scale of the Labour losses was such as to undermine the position of hitherto long-entrenched Labour councillors and of the traditional right-wing leadership which had dominated many Labour-controlled authorities. In some cases they had run both their councils and their local Labour parties in a somewhat secretive fashion, largely oblivious of such issues as public access to information and none too keen on opening up their party branches to new members who might prove to be an unknown quantity. The enormity of their defeat effectively knocked the bottom out of their world; some of them drifted out of politics in despair whilst those who remained were now vulnerable for perhaps the first time in their political lives. In Islington the three years after 1968 were dominated by 'a battle between different elements of the party for control of it and, more importantly, for control of the ward selection processes for council candidates' (Baine, 1975, p. 34). In Croydon 'many of the "old guard" who lost their seats that year never returned' (Saunders, 1980a, p. 227). Looking back on 1968 many year later Sheffield's David Blunkett (1982, p. 56) recognized that 'that year was traumatic. It began a shift in attitudes as well as in politics'.

The shift in attitudes was to take time; but it was also people, as well as attitudes, that changed. Thus, when the next elections occurred in the London boroughs in 1971 the newly returned Labour groups which reclaimed power in boroughs such as Islington, Lambeth and Wandsworth were seen to be a 'New Guard', 'Young Turks', 'a youthful meritocracy', in contrast to the 'Old Guard' who had vanished in the wreckage of 1968 (cf. Harrington, 1971). Even in Conservative Croydon the minority Labour group elected in 1971 was 'relatively young, inexperienced, and in many cases radical' (Saunders, 1980a, p. 227). The newcomers were by no means in the mould of the extra-parliamentary left of the late 1970s. Their concern for a rather more open style of government, for environmental issues, and for a more managerial approach to local decision-making did however differentiate them from their predecessors of the old Labour right. Nevertheless, they were far from being committed to extra-parliamentary politics and in some individual cases the logic of their politics was to lead them eventually into the SDP: thus Gerry Southgate, Labour's deputy leader in Islington in 1971, emerged as leader of the borough's short-lived SDP majority group in the winter of 1981/2. Appropriately enough, in view of the SDP's declared aspirations, individuals such as Southgate in 1971 were indeed helping to 'break the mould' of their time, for the emergence of the new guard Labour councillors of that year did reflect one important fact: the elections of 1967 and 1968 had in places effectively destabilized a pattern of local Labour politics that had persisted in some cases for a generation. The resulting fluidity was to facilitate the progress of the new urban left as it embarked on its activity in local government in later years.

Reorganization

Significant though they were, the local election defeats of 1967 and 1968 were not the only events to provoke a rupture in the established patterns of Labour's local government politics. The reform of local government outside Greater London in the early 1970s proved to be the occasion for a further break with previous practice.

One major feature of the reform was a sharp reduction in the number of councillors serving on the newly created authorities. Thus those Labour councillors who had survived the disasters of the late 1960s now found themselves potentially competing with each other, and with new aspirants, for a reduced number of winnable seats. Some simply retired from the fray with greater or lesser grace; others found themselves rejected in the selection process. Detailed accounts of these events are not available, but it seems particularly likely that many of the more elderly Labour aldermen, already long removed from the rigours of electioneering, were among those who vanished from the scene voluntarily or otherwise.

In some of the major metropolitan areas the scramble for seats was to some extent eased by the introduction of two-tier local government in places which had hitherto been single-tier county boroughs. However although this particular reform may have created more openings for would-be councillors it also simultaneously created more would-be councillors. Under the county borough system many Labour Party members were debarred from serving as councillors because they worked for the only council within whose boundary they lived. Once these authorities were reconstructed on a two-tier basis then it became possible for such people to seek election to whichever of the two councils was not their employer. This opened up new avenues in particular for teachers and college and polytechnic lecturers and also for local government officers themselves who could now aspire to dual roles as officers and politicians on separate authorities. As Elcock (1981, p. 446) has suggested such people often turned out to be loath 'to submit willingly to autocratic leadership or to accept without question a policy line set out *ex cathedra* by their Leader'. Such attitudes were clearly incompatible with the perpetuation of some of the practices of the old-style Labour 'city bosses'; they thus heralded the emergence of a more democratic, or at least more consultative, style of Labour group leadership and thus one more responsive to events not only within the group but also within the party outside the council.

The organization of the party outside the council was also undergoing reform at this time in order to align it more closely with the new local authority structure. In particular the old city party organizations, which were in practice often dominated by councillors, disappeared in the general move towards a system of district and county parties each securely based on representation from ward branches and constituency parties. (In the London boroughs Labour Party local government committees already performed similar functions to those of district parties elsewhere.) In addition a number of amendments were eventually made in 1984 to the party's model standing orders for Labour groups to ensure greater liaison between groups and local parties. Such reforms, combined with official party discouragement of councillors holding office in district or county parties, meant that Labour groups could not take for granted the acquiescence of the local party in all they did. Although much depended on the energy and views of local district and county party delegates the latter were now in a stronger position to try and influence councillors. Even so there were some who sought a more decisive influence for the party over its councillors but their attempts in the early 1980s to alter the model standing orders in the direction of greater party control rather than simply better liaison were not successful. In a number of cases however local practices were adopted which went a long way towards involving local parties in Labour group decision-making, although strictly speaking they were sometimes in contravention of the party's rules.

The issue of relations between Labour groups and their local party organizations had come to the fore mainly because of disputes over how best to react to the local government legislation introduced by the Conservative government after the general election of 1979. This legislation, and the spending cuts which accompanied it, were bitterly opposed within the Labour Party. However some differences of view as to how that opposition should be conducted soon began to emerge, initially during the battle over the Local Government Planning and Land Act 1980.

Opposing the cuts

In the battle over the 1980 Act Labour's spokesmen in Parliament and on the local authority associations took their stand firmly on the principle of defending the rights of local authorities to take their own decisions. This had certain implications for internal party arrangements, as Roy Hattersley, the then front bench Environment spokesman, pointed out on a number of occasions. If Labour was opposing the government's legislation on the grounds that elected councils should be allowed to decide for themselves, then by the same token nobody should try to impose any uniform policy on all Labour groups. Time and again Hattersley reiterated this point. At the party's 1980 local government conference for example he asserted that 'the party nationally cannot lay down any rigid rules . . . It would be wholly inconsistent with our belief in and defence of local autonomy.' At the party's annual conference that same year his message was the same: 'The policy of this party is for freedom and autonomy in local government. Local councils acting honourably as Socialist councillors can make their own decisions about what is right for the area they represent.' However, there were those in the party for whom local government autonomy was not in itself the crucial issue. For them the fight was not about the proper rights, duties and mutual relations of central and local government but about the Conservative attempt to dismantle the infrastructure of the welfare state and thereby undermine the living standards of the working class. If this contest was to be won, then it required a united stand by Labour councils. Ted Knight, leader of Lambeth Council and a leading proponent of this view, put it thus at Labour's 1979 annual conference:

> And if . . . you are going to defend the living standards of working people in Britain, then, frankly the Labour movement cannot carry out the cuts. We have got to stand firm. And if Labour authority after Labour authority throughout London, the metropolitan areas and the country as a whole was to stand firm, then we can thrust back the Tory offensive.

Knight was not alone in his views. An emergency resolution was carried at the 1980 annual conference which instructed the NEC

> to co-ordinate a united fight of Labour Councils and trade unions on a firm no cuts position . . . Delay will see the destruction of social programmes which have taken decades to build up.

Thus although Labour's leaders in Parliament and in the local authority associations were concerned with both the constitutional issue and the expenditure issue, there were those to the left of them for whom the former was something of a sideshow. They saw the battle over 'the destruction of social programmes' as the key struggle. Their plea was for leadership from the NEC in that struggle, and the purpose of that leadership would be to ensure unity in order to defeat the government. The demands for leadership and unity which emerged during the battles over the 1980 Act were reiterated as the Thatcher government pressed ahead with its assaults on local government during the early 1980s. They became particularly insistent as the government went ahead with its plans for rate-capping and for abolition of the GLC and the metropolitan counties after its election victory in 1983.

However, the plea for leadership from the NEC came up against a major stumbling-block, namely the practical inability of the NEC to secure concerted action amongst local Labour groups due to the absence of any suitable machinery within the party's constitution. One set of reasons why it was not possible for the NEC to direct Labour groups to respond in a particular way was articulated very clearly by Neil Kinnock at a protest meeting in Westminster Hall in November 1979. Responding, as a member of the NEC and of its cuts campaign sub-committee, to demands from the floor for a lead from the NEC, he replied:

> Local Labour groups are autonomous. We [the NEC] can appeal, we can advise, we can point out the political consequences. In public speeches we can make great appeals . . . but Labour groups must take their cases one by one.

Moreover, it was Labour councillors, not the NEC, who stood to incur penalties for overspending. It would, Kinnock argued, be quite wrong for someone like him to be marching councillors into battle and then 'offering to hold the coats'.

Whether wrong or not it would in fact have been a constitutional impossibility, for nowhere does the party's constitution, or its model standing orders for Labour groups, provide any mechanism for making those groups accountable to the national level of the party, whether at headquarters or at Westminster, or indeed to annual conference. A relationship of consultation and exhortation is all that can be achieved.

However the question of the party's rules and standing orders was only part of the difficulty: just as intractable was the matter of what substantive policies should be pursued by Labour-controlled councils in the face of Conservative government policy. Calls for a lead from the NEC and for a united front of Labour councils did not in themselves address two other important questions – around what particular agreed strategy was unity to be forged or leadership provided? and was this strategy to be merely a defensive one of protecting those 'social programmes which have taken decades to build up' or did it have some more positive role to play?

The NEC's first attempt, in 1980, to provide some sort of strategy for Labour councils, in the form of a statement *Councils and the Cuts*, was one which gave the uneasy appearance of trying to square the circle. While it called for a 'united approach to the formulation of policy decisions by Labour-controlled councils' it also recognized that 'there are real differences in local circumstances and that councils must make their own judgements'. It urged Labour councils 'to refuse to implement government policy': yet it also identified those services which it would 'strongly advise Labour-controlled councils especially . . . to maintain' which sounded like an exercise, not in defiance, but in damage limitation.

The 1980 statement met with a mixed and largely sceptical reaction from all wings of the party and thereafter individual Labour councils were in practice left to discover their own salvation. Some looked for the least painful cuts and attempted to put any blame on to the Conservative government; others simply raised the rates to compensate for grants foregone but after a while that became less and less attractive as the burden of rates on working-class households rose. Some use was made of 'creative accountancy' and other forms of financial ingenuity though this often merely served to postpone the evil day. In some instances a strategy of 'majority opposition' was contemplated, though never adopted, whereby a majority Labour group would refuse to take office but would obstruct their opponents' attempts to do so, in an attempt to paralyse the workings of the authority and so force a confrontation with the government. Mass resignation of Labour councillors followed by a series of by-elections to renew Labour's mandate was also suggested, though only the GLC, with four such by-elections in 1984, came near to taking up this strategy. The most radical policy to be pursued was that adopted by Liverpool in 1984 which delayed the making of a rate for some months until it had secured from the government some minor financial concessions which it then presented, inaccurately, as a substantial victory.

The Liverpool policy might have been seen as an isolated initiative from a far-left council. However, after the re-election of the Conservative government in 1983, the introduction of legislation to introduce rate-capping and the threatened abolition of the metropolitan counties and of the GLC were seen as a clear escalation of the attack on local government in general and on Labour councils in particular and led to a more widespread willingness to contemplate more drastic acts of non-compliance. Labour's local government conference at Nottingham in February 1984 was pervaded by a sense that some major confrontation could not be long postponed, with the party chairman, Eric Heffer, even reminding delegates of the fiftieth anniversary of the destruction of 'Red' Vienna by the guns of the rightist Dollfuss government in 1934. A few months later the conference met again at Sheffield in a recall session out of which there emerged considerable agreement on a future strategy of non-compliance with government proposals for rate-capping.

The basis of the strategy lay in a document prepared by the Labour leaders of the GLC and seven London boroughs and stating that:

We resolve not to comply with any cuts in expenditure levels with the resultant impact in services and jobs. This objective can best be achieved by ensuring the maximum degree of unity between Labour controlled authorities in resisting the Government, although we recognise that differing local circumstances may mean that different tactics will have to be adopted. We shall not seek derogation – that is, redetermination of expenditure levels, because of the loss of local financial autonomy and control of services.

As the only focal point around which all rate-capped and potentially rate-capped authorities can unite is at the stage of budget and rate-making, our preferred option is to make a budget which protects services and jobs, but to refuse to make a rate until the Government has restored Rate Support Grant, so that services can be protected without the need for unacceptable rate rises.

The document met with considerable support within the conference and its terms were thereafter conveyed by Eric Heffer to the NEC who went on to endorse the policy of non-compliance. This chain of events was particularly significant in a number of ways.

First, after calling in vain for leadership from the NEC and the parliamentary party, the leaders of the 'front-line' Labour councils had finally filled the leadership vacuum themselves with a commitment to a specific course of action. Second, the local government conference, dominated, unlike the full party conference, by local councillors and party activists, had, despite its formal lack of any decision-making powers, been used effectively as a means of policy initiation. Third, the NEC had swiftly moved to endorse a policy of defending local government which embraced non-compliance and the clear possibility of confrontation with central government. These events reflected partly the sense that Labour in local government was rapidly approaching a last-ditch defence position but also, adversity notwithstanding, a growing sense of self-confidence about the role and relevance of local government within Labour's strategy. This had been symbolized perhaps by the election of David Blunkett to the NEC in October 1983 and by the subsequent elevation of the NEC's local government sub-committee to full committee status on a par with the Home Policy and International Policy Committees. There was moreover a sense that despite the overwhelming Conservative majority in the House of Commons, Labour had been winning much of the argument and much of the battle of public opinion on local government issues. In terms of taking the fight to the enemy and of maintaining party morale local government had become something of a jewel in Labour's crown.

Even so, it had been recognized for some time that a merely defensive campaign was not enough in itself. In 1980 SERA had stressed the need 'to link current campaigns against the cuts with debate about long-term ideas on the reform of local government, decentralisation and news of constructive action on economic and environmental issues' (*SERA News*, Summer 1980). To defend local government successfully was seen to require measures to improve and to change the way it operated. 'Some socialist councillors are now arguing that they can build support to defend local government if they can provide the services which people want . . . [but] not all the old structures are worth defending' (Massey *et al.*, 1984, p. 19). After all 'no one will easily defend a socialist principle (like for example direct labour) if it is encapsulated in a service (like council housing repairs) which is paternalistic, authoritarian or plain inefficient' (Blunkett and Green, 1984, p. 2). Thus defending local government would also involve using it 'to create an administration which might prefigure a wider socialist society' (ibid.). Local socialism needed therefore to embrace pre-figurative as well as defensive strategies; it should 'mobilise the community in defence of itself and positively in favour of the new way forward' (Blunkett, 1981a). It is the sources of that 'new way forward' that we may now explore.

Movements and ideas

Community action

The various developments within the Labour Party from the late 1960s onwards did not occur in a vacuum. In the wider world of politics and social movements there were a number of events occurring in the same period which were to play their part in the emergence of local socialism in particular and of a belief in a decentralized form of socialism in general. In some cases these developments can be seen as being, at least in part, a reflection of some of Labour's own internal problems. This is true for example of the emergence of the community action movement, some of whose origins lay in disillusion with the Labour Party yet whose development was ultimately to lead many of its members to try once again to find in Labour a vehicle for their aspirations.

Community action was described by Richard Crossman (1977, p. 126) as a process of encouraging a local community to 'pull itself up by its own bootstraps': as such it was heir to the tradition of community development in Britain's colonial empire. But if it was 'about people in deprived areas looking at their own problems and seeking their own solutions' (Baine, 1975, p. 17) it was also more than an exercise in localized self-help drawing on traditions of colonial development or community work. 'Community workers who entered the field in the late 1960s and early 1970s largely rejected the traditional models of community work practice . . . [in favour of] a commitment to organising and a willingness to use conflict strategies to achieve their objectives' (Loney, 1983, pp. 23–4). While willing to use conventional strategies of bargaining, persuading and cajoling to secure results, 'the distinguishing feature of community action [was] its refusal to stick to such tactics if they [did] not produce results' (Baine, 1975, p. 30). This implied a highly politicized mode of operation, challenging established patterns of influence and resources, yet this politicization lay outside the boundaries of the conventional left-wing politics of the day.

The Notting Hill Summer Project of 1967 is often seen as the birthplace of British community action. Its presuppositions were compared favourably with those of the Labour Party:

> To the Labour party the main problem was how to win (or lose as well as possible) the next election – here the problem was poverty and bad housing and lack of amenities. To the Labour party people were ticks on a canvass register – here they were to be central to the solution of their own problem. For me, from then on, the Labour party was dead as a possible organisational form. The same was true of the hundreds of other young, and not so young, people who turned to the ideas of community action as a basis for their political life. (Baine, 1975, p. 10)

Dissatisfaction with the Labour Party was a common theme among radical community activists in the late 1960s (Silburn and Coates, 1970; Lapping, 1970; O'Malley, 1977). It was a time when 'radical optimism', fired by the 'events' of 1968, 'was coupled with a pervasive scepticism . . . about traditional organisations and political parties of the left' (Mayo, 1979, p. 132); Labour's membership was declining and its organization in working-class areas seemed in danger of withering away (Whiteley, 1982; Hindess, 1971). 'The radical community workers saw in . . . the decline of the local ward Labour parties an opportunity to find a receptive constituency for militant action around local issues' (Loney, 1983, p. 24).

Seen by many, therefore, as an alternative to the Labour Party for radical politics, community action was itself to become further radicalized by the experience of the Community Development Projects (CDPs) set up by the central government in 1969 as one of a number of initiatives to combat urban poverty. This radicalization has been chronicled by Kraushaar (1979, 1981), Higgins et al. (1983) and Loney (1983). It arose partly through the ineptitude of the Home Office's direction of the projects, partly through the predispositions of radical activists working in some of the projects (e.g. North Tyneside, Benwell, Birmingham and Newham) and partly through the development of a network of inter-project organizations such as the Consultative Council, the CDP Workers' Organization, the CDP Political Economy Collective, and the CDP Information and Intelligence Unit, which enabled the exchange of experiences and ideas between projects. Loney (1983, p. 96) suggests that the Coventry CDP was an especially significant source of radical initiatives, having 'a considerable impact on the future direction of CDP'. Coventry's particular contribution was to argue increasingly from 1972 onward 'that the CDP should shift its attention from the symptoms of deprivation and its victims, to its causes ... to a "structural" analysis of social problems' (Higgins *et al.*, 1983, p. 33). This broadening of horizons eventually applied not only to modes of understanding the problem but also to modes of dealing with it. By 1975 the Coventry CDP was arguing that 'the greatest potential for change may lie in new initiatives which create alliances across the neighbourhood, the factory floor, and the local political parties' (quoted in Loney, 1983, p. 151). One activist came to see the role of community action as 'contributing towards a movement that will eventually crystallise in new political formations. I don't know whether that means new political parties or a reformulation of the Labour Party for instance' (quoted in Kraushaar, 1981, p. 118).

A certain 'reformulation' of the Labour Party was, however, already under way, with the left gaining increasing ground, organizationally and ideologically, throughout the 1970s. Such a Labour Party was therefore increasingly congenial to those who had written it off in and after 1968; accordingly it forced community activists to face once again one of 'the old intractable problems of the political left', namely whether to work from within the Labour Party or outside it (Baine, 1975, p. 96). By 1979 Mayo (1979, pp. 141–2) could talk of a 'major shift of focus in community work' revolving around 'the whole issue of alliances with the mainstream of the Labour movement ... In retrospect it was the attempts to "go it alone" in the community in the late 1960s which were atypical – returning community work to the mainstream of labour movement politics fits into a more accurate historical view of working class politics.'

In any case, atypical or not, the strategy of 'going it alone' had not proved wholly successful. A review of the experience of the 1970s concluded that 'the record overall for the past few years has been as depressing as it is now ... in many areas of the country there have been few if any gains ... Few campaigning groups or federations have been kept strong for long.' The remedy for the weakness was seen to be in shifting activity 'from focusing on tenants and community groups to the range of organisations in the broader labour movement ... Building strength and unity in the labour movement has to be the basis of the fight back' (*Community Action*, September/October 1980).

The rapprochement between community action and Labour politics took a variety of forms. In some localities alliances with radical Labour MPs and councillors were sought in order to 'legitimise' CDP campaigns (Loney, 1983, p. 183); in certain instances CDP analyses began to leave their mark in Labour local election manifestos (Sharman, 1981). A number of individuals with a record of community activism emerged as major figures in Labour council politics – such as GLC committee chairmen George Nicholson and Michael Ward, while others took up positions as officers with left Labour authorities – for example Geoff Green (ex-Birmingham CDP) in Sheffield's Central Policy Unit and Nick Sharman (ex-Benwell and Joint Docklands Action Group) in the GLC's Enterprise Board.

The experience of community action and its participants was summed up by Loney in the following terms:

> The millennial visions which carried student radicals into poor neighbourhoods in the late 1960s and early 1970s had been replaced by the end of the decade with a more low key but realistic strategy for action within working class areas.

This new strategy was however 'accompanied by an increasingly sophisticated theory of the state' (Loney, 1983, p. 161).

Theorizing

The gradual replacement of 'going it alone' by a more measured strategy of action within, or in alliance with, the Labour Party, was not merely a shift at the level of practice. It was also accompanied by attempts at a clearer and more subtle theoretical understanding of the nature of the state which was no longer dismissed outright as the 'executive committee of the bourgeoisie'.

The significance of such theorizing lay in the rationale it provided for bridging the gap between local government and community action. In particular it allowed the co-existence of an 'insistence on an underlying structural analysis' with a justification for not 'folding your arms' and waiting 'till a kind of left-wing God sends you a revolution' (Kraushaar, 1979, p. 63). If, as Loney suggests (1981, p. 66), much CDP writing represented 'an attempt to come to grips with the changing nature of the state and with the implications of theory for radical practice' then in doing so it opened the way for the attempted use of the local state for radical ends.

Theorizing about the local state was not of course confined to radical community activists. In 1969 Miliband's *The State in Capitalist Society* marked the start of a new debate amongst Marxists about the nature of the state. The question of whether the state should be seen as functioning purely to meet the requirements of capital accumulation or whether it was better conceived as an arena of class struggle became a key element of the debate. In 1977 Cockburn's *The*

Local State inserted into this debate the issue of the nature and role of local government.

The significance of the debate for those involved in local political and community activism was that out of it there emerged some sort of intellectual or ideological rationale for radical action short of violent revolution. In particular, in so far as it provided alternatives to a crude determinism it promoted views such as those of the activist who said that

> I don't see the state . . . as necessarily functioning in a deterministic way purely in the interests of capital or the working class. I see the state as part of a battle, in the centre of the arena, between ruling-class and working-class interests. (Quoted in Kraushaar, 1979, p. 75)

For another activist, too, recognition of 'the relative autonomy of the state and the contradictions which exist within and between different layers of government and indeed within the ruling class itself' was important because it suggested a 'space' within which radicals could manoeuvre, not least in challenging the ideological, as well as the economic, subordination of the working class (Mayo, 1979, pp. 136–7). This 'relative autonomy' was important not only because it abandoned the notion of a state which was merely the 'executive committee of the bourgeoisie' but also because it embraced the possibility that the local level of the state might itself possess a certain degree of autonomy from the central state. Some theorists began to see the local state as having a certain functional specificity of its own, and also a certain degree of open-ness and accessibility to popular pressure which distinguished it from the central state (Cawson and Saunders, 1983). The latter idea echoed the Labour Co-ordinating Committee's assertion (1981, p. 15) that, for all its faults, the existence of local government meant that 'power is therefore distributed more widely than the central state machine and can be used as a counter-weight to corporatist tendencies'. It became increasingly true to say, with Corrigan (1979, p. 203), that the concept of the local state and the debates which surrounded it came to 'enter into the everyday language of socialists' inside and outside the Labour Party (cf. 'Breaking Up the Local State', *London Labour Briefing*, August 1982).

It is unlikely that all activists, busy as they were, addressed themselves in detail to all the nuances of the debate about the local state, though one should not underestimate the importance which many of them attached to a correct theoretical underpinning to their work. Nevertheless the debate, and particularly the concepts and the language which it developed, provided a means of assimilating localized community action into the broader framework of socialist and Labour movement politics. It also provided a rationale for Labour leftists to involve themselves in a local government world which, so long as its direct relevance to class politics was unclear, they had hitherto left largely to more centrist and rightist comrades.

Economics, environmentalism and feminism

Paralleling the growing concern over the nature and potential of the local state was a similar interest in the working of local economies and their relationships with the wider national and international economy. The various CDP reports 'underlined again and again the overwhelming importance of the local economy' to the conditions of community life; moreover their attempts to link the fortune of local communities to the workings of the economy as a whole 'had considerable influence during the 1970s within community work and more generally among Labour movement activists' (Sharman, 1981, p. 142; cf. Ward, 1981). The development of a 'political economy of urbanism' was not only significant in putting economic issues on to the agenda of local politics. Because of its concern with, amongst other things, the role of the state in restructuring the economy, it also brought the debate about the local economy into conjunction with the debate about the local state. One practical result was the establishment of a number of locally oriented labour and community research and resource centres concerned with 'common community problems like de-industrialisation, new technology, unemployment, housing decay and local economic and social decline' and with understanding the links 'between the issues faced by people in their workplace, homes or in the community' (Benington, 1981, p. 17).

Beyond the confines of the local economy, the problems of the national economy in the 1970s also had certain implications. Thus one writer concluded that the experience of the 1974–9 Labour government had shown that 'attempts to use central State structures as a means of facilitating socialist change in economic organisation have been inadequate' (Ward, 1981, p. 13). The 1979–80 Trades Council Inquiry into *State Intervention in Industry* had come to a similar conclusion, and had identified the need for a socialist government to be based 'on a source of political power outside the existing state. Our conclusion, then, is that working class people will have to build up their own forms of political power' (Coventry, Liverpool, Newcastle and North Tyneside Trades Councils, 1980, p. 147). This view was echoed in a paper delivered at a Labour Co-ordinating Committee conference in 1981 in which it was argued that 'the failures experienced by both central and local government alike in the course of relatively centralised planning and direction suggest more grass roots involvement is a precondition of success' (Ashton, 1981, p. 8).

There thus emerged during the 1970s a body of experience and ideas, focusing on the community, on the local state and on the economy which attached considerable importance to political action for socialist ends at the local level and which was prepared to see local political activity as being at least as relevant as politics directed at the national or central government level, if not more so. Further support for such strategies was forthcoming from the environmentalist movement and from the women's movement.

It was SERA which launched the bi-monthly news letter *Local Socialism* in April 1980, aiming to link up the various debates about opposing spending cuts, decentralization, the local economy, and environmental issues. One argument which explicitly linked environmentalism and decentralized politics was expressed later by Alan Taylor in *SERA News* (Summer 1981):

Environmental degradation is largely the result of power being in the hands of people who do not suffer from the environmental consequences of their decisions. Economic activity is remotely owned and remotely controlled . . . If we are serious about the environment, then we should be serious about taking power away from the controllers of capital, and putting it in the hands of labour and in the hands of consumers and local communities.

In addition to environmentalism the women's movement has also been identified as contributing to the development of 'alternative styles of organisation . . . less formality and bureaucracy' (Ward, 1981, p. 14). Certainly one of the seminal works of the women's movement, *Beyond the Fragments*, contained a vigorous attack on authoritarian and elitist tendencies amongst left-wing groups and warned of the dangers of merely transmuting capitalist hierarchies into socialist hierarchies.

One of its co-authors, Hilary Wainwright, later to become a member of the GLC Economic Policy Group, emphasized the importance of 'the necessary preliminaries of raising and extending socialist consciousness and grass-roots organisation among the majority of working people' rather than concentrating on seizing governmental or state power, while another, Lynne Segal, spoke of the need not only to defend state welfare services but also to transform them 'not necessarily in a centralised form'. For Sheila Rowbotham one particular importance of feminism was that it had been 'the main organisational form through which pre-figurative politics had begun to influence the contemporary left' whereby 'self-help community activity . . . can indicate ways of questioning the role of professionals and the means of creating more direct forms of control over welfare resources' (Rowbotham *et al.*, 1979, pp. 2, 179, 138, 137).

It has been possible thus far to identify a number of individual bodies of experiences and ideas which provided some of the strands out of which local socialism came to be woven. Yet over and above these various particular elements it is possible to identify a more general and a more fundamental factor which made a decentralized local socialism seem an attractive proposition to so many activists. I have already referred to the new left's attempt to find a different road to socialism from those offered by the parliamentary and insurrectionary routes. Yet the problem was in fact more than one of strategy, of selecting the best way forward: in the eyes of some the destination was at least as problematic as the journey.

A new socialism?

'The very idea of socialism has been discredited for millions by the failures of social democracy and the history of the Soviet Union, Eastern Europe and China.' This harsh verdict came not from any propagandist of the new right but from a recruiting leaflet of the Socialist Society, formed early in 1982 with the aim of 'forging links between the new Labour left and socialists outside the party', in order to 'give concrete shape to the idea of a socialist alternative'. Such a verdict from inside the socialist camp reflected that 'deep crisis affecting both contemporary socialist thought and socialist movements' which some have traced to 'ambiguities and contradictions in the primordial socialist message' and not merely to 'contingent historical circumstances' (Kolakowski, 1977, p. 1).

The view of socialism as an ideal betrayed by its supposed adherents and rejected by its supposed beneficiaries, found wide and sometimes brutal expression by many from both East and West who still held fast to the promise, no matter how problematic the reality. At the first national congress of Polish Solidarity in 1981, for example, the reality of Communist rule was summed up by the socialist economist Edward Lipinski as 'this socialism of rotting economy, this socialism of prisoners, censorship and police' (Garton-Ash, 1983, pp. 225–6). The Yugoslav theoretician, Markovic (1982, p. ix) summarized the Communist experience as one in which 'Socialism became a synonym of State-rule over the whole of social life . . . an iron hand, and it ruled mercilessly . . . The battle-cry of revolutionaries: "Socialism or barbarism" was given an effective reply: "Socialism *is* barbarism. Socialism *is* Gulag" ' (emphasis in original). In France during the 1970s both Socialists and Communists made major reappraisals of Western and Eastern forms of socialism. 'Their critique encompassed all aspects of state power, including bureaucracy (oppressive), parties (bureaucratic), planning (disappointing), nationalization (more bureaucracy), [and] social welfare programs (administering capitalism)' (Brown, 1982, p. 26).

Nearer home, the legacy of British Labour was described in *Tribune* (9 July 1982) by one left-wing activist, Nigel Williamson, as one in which 'many of those who should benefit from what should be the greatest successes of British socialism to date – public ownership, the welfare state, municipal housing – actually regard these "successes" as part of the general force which is oppressing them'. Ken Livingstone (1982) similarly expressed the fear that 'those services which many of us in the Labour Party ... fought for are increasingly seen by those who receive them as instruments of control over their daily lives'. The equation of socialism with centralization and state control was identified as one of the electoral *Liabilities of the Left* in a pamphlet of that title written in the wake of the 1979 election defeat by a subsequent editor of *Local Socialism* (Anderson, 1979). These fears were echoed by individuals such as Peter Hain (1980a, p. 203), who regretted that socialism had 'become too identified with top heavy decision-making, with bureaucracy and alienation'. The Labour Party's further defeat in 1983 provoked similar reactions. Thus in July 1983 *London Labour Activist*, the journal of the London Labour Co-ordinating Committee, called for 'a thoughtful post-mortem and a new vision of socialism' and contrasted 'the past paternalism of right-wing Labourism's welfare state' with the future need 'for real decentralisation of decision-making in all spheres'.

Disillusion with existing models of socialism in its turn promoted attempts to suggest alternatives which would avoid the pitfalls previously encountered. Most of the alternative forms of socialism which have been canvassed in this context share a commitment to greater democracy and decentralization although they often differ from one another in certain respects. Socialists with experience of the planned economies of Eastern Europe have for example often combined calls for greater worker participation in industry and for political decentralization with proposals for greater use of the market mechanism. Thus, for example, exiled veterans of the Prague Spring of 1968 developed proposals for forms of market socialism in which socially owned and worker-managed enterprises would compete in a free market within certain broad parameters of planning (Sik, 1976; Selucky, 1979): similar views have been expressed by the Polish trade union Solidarity. In the West there has perhaps been less emphasis on the potential of the market and more concern for industrial democracy, workers' co-operatives and decentralization of the welfare state. In France the Socialist Party embraced the principle of *autogestion*, defined in the party's 1980 *Projet Socialiste* as the 'social state that will permit responsible men and women to decide whatever they please for themselves and the collectivity where they live and work, and with every form of centralism and gigantism broken' (quoted in Brown, 1982, p. 46). *Autogestion* has in fact been on the political agenda of the French left ever since the events of May 1968. In the 1970s it gave rise to what might be seen as a French equivalent of local socialism in the form of the *groupes d'action municipale* who gained some successes at local elections on programmes advocating more direct democracy in municipal affairs. After the electoral victory of the French Socialist Party in 1981 decentralization in such spheres as local government, hospital administration, policing and the arts became government policy, although *autogestion* in industry made little or no progress.

In Britain during and after the 1970s there was also a growing interest within the Labour Party in the problems of enhancing the democratic content of socialism with concepts such as public participation and industrial democracy being much in vogue. Under the 1974–9 Labour government the Bullock Report on Industrial Democracy was commissioned, the Co-operative Development Agency was created and an Industrial Common Ownership Act was passed. Criticisms of unresponsive bureaucracy and of excessive concentrations of power were voiced by leading Labour politicians, including Harold Wilson (1973) and Tony Benn (1980 and 1981), and a body of literature emerged which explored various interpretations and combinations of industrial democracy, workers' control, co-operatives and decentralization (Coates, 1976; Meacher, 1979; Radice, 1979; Taylor, 1980; Hain, 1980a and 1983; Hodgson, 1984). The relationship of local government to decentralist socialism was also examined, both in terms of its place in a strategy of socialist advance and of its role in pre-figuring possible elements of a socialist society (Blunkett, 1981b; Taylor, 1982; Donnison, 1983; Blunkett and Green, 1984; Seabrook, 1984; Wright *et al.*, 1984).

In view of such developments both in Britain and elsewhere it is possible to see that local socialism is not an isolated or esoteric phenomenon but represents part of a much broader trend. It is in fact one component of a widespread search for a 'socialism of a different kind' (Brown, 1982). Local socialism in Britain represents one particular contribution to that search. Its own ultimate impact on the wider development of socialist theory and practice has yet to be seen. But its immediate impact on the day-to-day workings of local government has been quite striking.

3 Local Government's Cultural Revolution

At the first meeting of the Labour group, there was a baby and cans of Coke. Senior officers found it a great upheaval. (Maurice Stonefrost, Director-General of the GLC, *Sunday Times*, 16 September 1984)

The top echelons of the bureaucracy have got to be politically aware. It does mean their jobs are insecure. That is the price people at the top have to pay. (Patrick Kodikara, Assistant Director of Social Services for Tower Hamlets and Chair of the Social Services Committee in Hackney, speaking after his appointment as Director of Social Services for Camden, *New Society*, 1 November 1984)

For many local government officers who had grown accustomed to a largely non-ideological form of local politics, the coming to power of the new urban left provided a severe case of culture shock. Councillors in jump suits and jeans; clenched fist salutes in the council chamber; the singing (and flying) of the Red Flag; employees wearing CND badges; office walls decorated with political posters and cartoons; disdain for many established practices and procedures; a frame of reference which gave party and ideology pre-eminence over professional considerations; the arrival of what Ken Livingstone described as 'people with a basic radical contempt for existing bureaucratic structures ... who were willing to kick a lot of backsides' (*Standard*, 23 March 1984): such phenomena and the reactions to them of some local government officers were a measure of the gap between them and their new political masters on the left.

As for the latter their commitment to local government politics did not mean that they always liked what they found once they arrived in the council chamber. One Wandsworth councillor for example complained that 'the council no longer runs primarily in the interests of the local community but rather in the interests of the service class who dominate the huge upper and middle reaches of the town hall'. Such people might sometimes proclaim leftist views but their socialism was merely a plea for 'more public spending channelled through a growing bureaucracy (to whose fingers it often seems to stick)' (Jeffers, 1980, pp. 4–5). A newly elected member of the minority Labour group on Devon County Council expressed his indignation 'at the power, privilege and opulence expressed at

County Hall' and at the 'patronising condescension' of the officers (*Local Socialism*, September 1981). Brian Powell, leader of Walsall Council from 1980 to 1982, condemned local authorities for 'placing so many obstacles in people's way, so many diversions and irrelevancies, that people can't find their way through the maze': his colleague Dave Church feared that in the eyes of the council 'you're not a human being any more, you're housing list applicants waiting for units of accommodation' (quoted in Seabrook, 1984, pp. 137 and 1).

For those who had a history of involvement in community action or in single-issue protest groups such attitudes were commonplace. Over the years they had come to see the professional bureaucrats and the elected politicians of local government as the enemy, as people to be confronted, challenged, circumvented and outwitted. The literature of community action – for example *Community Action* magazine – was and is replete with discussions of the most effective ways of organizing, lobbying, petitioning, publicizing and demonstrating in order to force councils to acknowledge and deal with problems which had been ignored or left unsolved. As for the ideas of community action, they

> deny the legitimacy of the councillor . . . they deny the validity of the expertise of the professional officers and they concentrate on change and innovation at the cost of the status quo. In all this they produce problems for the established structure. (Baine, 1975, p. 31).

It is therefore hardly surprising that Labour councillors with backgrounds of community activism should not worry unduly if some of their initiatives were to cause 'problems for the established structure' of local government. But even those who lacked that particular pedigree were often sceptical if not downright hostile towards the conventional workings of local authorities. A desire to defend the services that local government provided; a recognition that local government might provide Labour with a useful stage on which to regain ground lost in the parliamentary struggle with Thatcherism; a belief in the need for a less centralized form of socialism: none of these entailed any particular enthusiasm for the normal routines of local authority work. Indeed defending services, rebuffing Mrs Thatcher and devising a new approach to socialism might all require some clear departure from what had thus far been the orthodoxy of local government.

New issues

One very clear departure was recognizable in the way in which the left placed new issues on the agendas of local authorities or else transformed old issues almost beyond recognition. A clear instance of the latter can be found in the case of local economic initiatives.

The local economy

Local authority involvement in this field does of course pre-date the emergence of local socialism. However, much of the activity undertaken by local government in earlier years focused on the provision of indirect, and sometimes direct, assistance to the private sector, particularly to small firms. Councils made money available, in the form of loans or grants, for capital, for land and for buildings; in some cases workshops and factory units were constructed by councils and firms were then attracted into them by concessionary rent levels. In some cases advisory bureaux for small businesses were set up and in general attempts were made to promote a 'sympathetic' environment in which private entrepreneurs could flourish.

To the left such private sector oriented strategies seemed inadequate and irrelevant. In the light of 500,000 job losses in the capital since 1961, the Labour manifesto for the 1981 GLC elections concluded that such strategies were 'plainly not enough to cope with the scale of London's industrial decline . . . The public sector will have to take an active role.' Similar views were being expressed elsewhere, for in June 1981 Sheffield became the first local authority to set up an Employment Department and an Employment Committee.

Sheffield's Employment Department was charged not only with promoting new industrial and commercial development and investment: its responsibilities were also to include assisting in the development of co-operatives, planning agreements and a local enterprise board, instigating new municipal enterprises, and creating jobs within the council through the Manpower Services Commission (MSC) programmes. The department and the Employment Committee between them were to be concerned not only with preventing further job losses and promoting the creation of new jobs: they were also to seek more democratic control over employment, both through industrial democracy and co-operative organization at the place of work and through social planning of industrial change within the city.

Such concern for the social and political, as well as for the purely economic, aspects of employment have been repeated in the case of the GLC. A report of the GLC's Industry and Employment Committee in July 1983 identified four major elements which formed part of a central aim of securing 'full employment of London's labour force in socially useful production'. One such element was primarily or directly economic in the form of intervention – through investment, property development or purchasing policy – either to support firms threatened with closure or to encourage new initiatives. Another however was concerned with promoting skills, with encouraging trade unionism and industrial democracy, and with anti-discrimination measures in respect of women and ethnic minorities. A third element embraced the development of new forms of industrial techniques – 'human-centred technology' – and of experimental forms of workplace organization. Finally the fourth element, 'Popular Planning', was focused on the involvement in policy formulation of workers and consumers in particular industrial sectors or localities. These various socio-political ambitions in the field of employment are naturally to be found in the guidelines drawn up for the Greater London Enterprise Board (GLEB), established by the GLC as a means of implementing the council's industrial strategy. In addition to its involvement in saving or creating jobs the board also 'gives a high priority to the encouragement of new forms of industrial ownership and control, and increasing workforce participation' as well as to 'identifying and developing new technological products which are socially useful, and linking ideas and expertise through "technology networks" ' (GLEB, 1984, p. 13).

Sheffield and the GLC have perhaps been more politically ambitious in their aspirations for local economic policy than have some other councils, such as the West Midlands, who share their other objectives of defending and creating employment. None the less the general evolution of policy in this field amongst radical Labour authorities seems clearly in the direction not only of greater public sector involvement in the local economy but also of contesting traditional assumptions about workplace organization and decision-making in the local economy.

Policing

A similar concern with challenging established habits of power and authority can be found in the case of policing. Here too is an area in which local government has previously had some involvement but where the left now seeks substantial departures from past practice.

Police forces outside London are each formally responsible to a police authority in the form of a committee composed of councillors and magistrates. In some cases the committee functions as a committee of a single county council; in other cases, as in Devon and Cornwall or the Thames Valley, a force covering two or more counties has a joint police committee to watch over it. The 'watch' however is conducted at something like arm's length and the committees have no control over operational decisions. In London itself the Metropolitan Police comes directly under the wing of the Home Secretary, there being no local government based police authority for the capital.

The London situation is clearly anomalous and was recognized as such by the Marshall Inquiry on Greater London in 1978 which called for the setting up in London of 'a Police Committee which would approve the police force budget and have a voice in the appointment of the Commissioner' (Marshall, 1978, para. 13.1). However a more general nationwide problem of police account-ability came to be identified in the late 1970s in the wake of increasing public concern over various aspects of crime, public order and policing.

During this period a number of aspects of police work began to give rise to public debate, most notably perhaps the effects of the disappearance of the 'beat bobby' and his replacement by patrol car policing during the 1960s. Of particular concern in liberal and socialist quarters were such issues as police–black relations, policing of demonstrations and industrial disputes, police interrogation practices and the role of the police in surveillance and security. Such concerns pre-dated the urban riots of the summer of 1981 but these events crystallized much of those anxieties about, and in some cases the antagonism towards, the police that already existed.

Within the Labour Party opinion expressed itself clearly at the 1981 annual conference. A resolution was passed committing the party to 'the introduction of effective democratic control' through the creation of police authorities whose powers would 'include the approval of all police policies, the appointment of senior officers, control over resources and manpower, training, disciplinary power and the development of police/community relations'. This conference resolution echoed the commitment which had been made in the GLC elections earlier in the year in Labour's manifesto, which called similarly for a police authority of elected members with 'power to appoint all officers of the rank of chief superintendent and above, to scrutinise the day-to-day affairs of the force and to allocate the resources to the various police functions'.

In the absence of a police authority of that nature radical Labour councils had to develop their own conception of a role in relation to policing. In those cases where there did exist a conventional police authority relations could become strained as councillors probed into, and commented publicly upon, police activities. This was true for example of Greater Manchester and of Merseyside which became perhaps the most notorious such case. There, in the aftermath of the 1981 riots, 'the Chief Constable displayed an attitude which verged on contempt for his police authority' (Scraton, 1982, p. 35) and the chairman of the authority concluded ironically that 'we have a system of workers' control of the police service far beyond anything that even the most revolutionary amongst us would dare to dream of' (Simey, 1982, p. 52).

In London, where there was no local police authority, some Labour councils set up their own police committees, the GLC in 1981 and ten of the boroughs in and after 1982, each of which developed its own agenda. Camden, for example, set up a police sub-committee of its Policy and Resources Committee in September 1982. In a report to the sub-committee in August 1984 the chairman, Robert Latham, characterized its function as one of providing 'an authoritative forum for debate about police in the Borough'. It had, he claimed, produced 'impartial and well-researched reports and information on areas of acute concern such as policing and the black–ethnic community, women, the gay community, the issue of fire arms to police, prostitution, the use of Stop and Search powers, the Police and Criminal Evidence Bill, crime and the media'. In the future he hoped that the committee would be able 'to evolve a systematic set of policing objectives that coincides with the real needs and wants of the community and that will have their backing'.

In 1983 the report of the Policy Studies Institute (PSI) research project on the Metropolitan Police was seen as confirming many of the concerns expressed by bodies such as the various London police committees. The report's recommendations related to desirable changes in police management and practice rather than to possible mechanisms for police accountability. It was however the research findings of the project which seemed to confirm the worst fears of the police committees. This was particularly true of the evidence of racism and sexism being endemic throughout the force. The findings that 'racialist language and racial prejudice were prominent and pervasive' (PSI, 1983, vol. IV, p. 109) and that 'the dominant values of the force are still in many ways those of an all-male institution' (op. cit., p. 91) were particularly disturbing to authorities who had identified race and women's issues as fields for political initiatives.

Race

Islington is one of the fourteen London boroughs which, together with the GLC and ILEA, had by June 1984 set up a race relations committee or sub-committee. The terms of reference of the Islington committee were set out in the council's standing orders as follows:

(i)   To initiate and develop policies in respect of all aspects of race relations in and affecting the Borough and its inhabitants and to establish the present and future needs of minority communities.

(ii) To ensure that the Council's policies and activities are non-discriminatory and to monitor their implementation by the Council's committees.

(iii) Where appropriate to take maximum advantage of grants, etc., available from central Government and other sources.

(iv) To provide advice and support to organisations on race relations matters.

(v) To engender co-operation and liaison with and between public authorities throughout the Borough on matters of race relations.

The aspirations contained in Islington's standing orders would be reflected in the terms of reference of other race relations committees, and of the supporting race relations units which existed in eight of the fourteen boroughs plus the GLC and ILEA. The placing of race on the local political agenda was the product of a variety of factors. They included pressure from community relations organizations, recognition of the electoral importance of ethnic minority voters, the impact of the 1981 riots and the emergence of black councillors in small but growing numbers especially within the Labour Party. As the Islington example shows the agenda entails action not only within the local community but also within the local authority. Thus Camden's Race Relations Unit sees one of its functions as being 'to look at the institutional racism in the Council itself' in addition to offering 'support and liaison with groups within the community providing grants and encouragement for self-help projects' (*Camden Magazine*, July 1984, pp. 11–12).

The struggle against racism is not seen as merely a matter of specific policies of encouragement and grant-funding or of implementing equal opportunity programmes through positive or affirmative action schemes or of racism awareness training within local authorities, important though these may be. The ultimate problem is that racism is not merely about prejudice, it is also about power. It is 'the power and ability to put into effect one's prejudice to the detriment of particular racial groups' (GLC, 1984).

Such a definition clearly carries the implication that 'racism is very much the result of white power [and that] the challenge to racism is inevitably aimed at the whites who hold the power'. One consequence of this in a local government system dominated by whites is that 'challenging bureaucratic elitism and local government professionalism are interwoven in the struggle against institutionalised racism' (Ouseley, 1984, pp. 155 and 144) since it is that same white-dominated elitism and professionalism which prevents local ethnic communities developing their full potential. This analysis matches fairly closely that which sees local authority hierarchies as being dominated not only by whites but also by males. Again, from this latter feminist perspective there comes another challenge to the established practices of local government.

Women's initiatives

By the autumn of 1984 twenty-two local authorities had set up women's committees in some form, thereby following the example of the GLC in 1982. The GLC committee had not been foreshadowed in the Labour manifesto at the 1981 GLC elections. It was not until early 1982 that the GLC Labour group endorsed Valerie Wise's proposal to form a GLC Women's Committee: the proposal had arisen out of discussions in 1981 over women's employment problems and grants to women's groups, each of which was being handled by a separate committee. In a sense this fragmentation of women's concerns was seen as symbolic of a wider marginalization of women in society at large. In the words of Valerie Wise who went on to chair the new committee: 'We are living in a man's world – a world designed by men for men where women have to fit in as best they can. Our aim is to change things – to change the way London is run so that the interests and welfare of women are equally important' (GLC, 1983a). Since women accounted for 52 per cent of London's population she looked 'towards a future where the provision of public services truly reflects the needs of the majority of the population in London – women' (letter to *The Times*, 18 February 1983). The example of the GLC in creating the committee was followed by other authorities including not only nine London boroughs but also major cities such as Leeds, Birmingham, Newcastle-upon-Tyne, Aberdeen and Edinburgh, not all of whom were strongholds of the new urban left.

A major concern of some of the committees was to make the business of political discussion and decision-making as accessible and informed as possible. This has involved varying patterns of open meetings and working groups, with co-options on to the actual women's committees from various quarters. Camden for example set up working groups on childcare, employment, social services, ethnic/black minority women, prostitution, health, women's rights, safety, disability, housing, arts and leisure and lesbianism. Its women's committee made provision for specific co-options from black/ethnic minorities, lesbians, trades unionists, the disabled and older women. Participation in meetings has been facilitated by the provision of creches, special facilities for the disabled, translations for Asian women and free transport. Such devices represent attempts to implement some of the principles of 'feminist democracy ... maximum involvement of the maximum number, non-hierarchical structures with a distribution of authority, rotation of tasks, sensitivity to different women's needs, abilities, development and competence, diffusion of information and equal access to resources' (Roelofs, 1983, p. 18).

The problems of implementing such a new style of politics have not been slow to emerge. In 1983 the GLC Women's Committee found itself under attack for insisting on its own ultimate powers of decision on issues taken up by its various working groups and open meetings, while some Labour group members were accused of being 'downright distrustful and unsupportive' (Clarke, 1983, p. 15). Within the London boroughs those to the north of the river found themselves generally more able than those to the south to draw on a reservoir of activists from previously existing feminist networks. The very openness of some of the procedures has sometimes meant that 'both the attendance and the decisions of these meetings shift from week to week . . . they can be and have been taken over by groups that are organised enough to hold caucus meetings in advance . . . [and they] must inevitably attract women who are articulate, who are used to, and able to, travel' (Goss, 1984, p. 127). These are not necessarily problems inherently peculiar to the politics of women; they are however more sharply focused by attempts to combine a very open and unstructured form of politics with attempts to 'make meetings accessible to inexperienced and unorganised women as well as the articulate and practised groups' (op. cit., p. 129).

New issues and old priorities

The local economy, policing, race and women's issues do not exhaust the new items which the left have placed on the agendas of their local authorities although they may have had the greatest impact in terms of creating new structures for decision-making and new demands for funding. Topics such as nuclear-free zones, Northern Ireland, Grenada and the rights of lesbians and gay men have also pre-occupied some new left councillors. One problem over which there has been a debate however is how much importance should be accorded to some of the new issues compared with the more traditional Labour priorities.

In Sheffield, for example, David Blunkett (1984, p. 255) has spoken of 'not wanting the women's issue to sap the energy of the class struggle generally' and the city council has no separate women's committee. In Liverpool the contrast between left politics there and in London was summed up by one councillor with the observation that 'Merseyside politics is not life-style politics'. The pressures of economic decline and the presence of an 'old left' and the *Militant* tendency have combined to subordinate issues of sexuality, women's rights and race to the imperatives of class politics. To the deputy chair of the city's Personnel Committee 'the reality of unemployment in Liverpool . . . is that we all share a common misery. Positive discrimination . . . would split the community right down the middle' (Dunlop, 1984, p. 9). Such attitudes however have not been accept-able to everyone on the left in Liverpool. Doubts amongst the black community about the strategy of the city council's Labour group eventually came to a head over the appointment of an alleged *Militant* supporter to the post of head of the council's race relations unit. In November 1984 demonstrators from the Liverpool Black Caucus opposing the appointment broke into and disrupted a city council meeting, hurling accusations of racism against the deputy leader and chair of the Personnel Committee, Derek Hatton. At a rally before the meeting Keva Coombes, leader of Merseyside County Council, who had earlier in the year publicly supported Liverpool in their financial battle with the government, had condemned the District Labour Party for its commitment to the appointment (*Liverpool Daily Post*, 15 November 1984).

In London also problems have been seen in accommodating the new issues to the old priorities, though not perhaps quite so starkly as in Liverpool. In a debate in *London Labour Briefing* in March 1984 Margaret Hodge, the leader of Islington Council, commented that 'activists in gay and lesbian politics come from a group whose social, occupational, educational and cultural background bears little resemblance to the population of the Inner City'. She was concerned about the 'very marked divergence between those active in [Labour] Women's Council and Sections and the growing number of women who are active in Tenants Associations' and about the need to 'prioritise basic bread and butter issues like the economic status of working-class women'.

Such problems of reconciling new issues and old priorities are more than matters of mere tactics. They go to the heart of one of the major elements of local socialism, namely that of welding together 'new' ethnic and cultural minorities and the 'old' working class through a politics of campaigning and mobilization. The strains and stresses of reconciling the traditions and the interests of the different groups pose major problems for the Labour Party: the mechanics of campaigning and mobilization also imply a new role, and new problems, for local authorities.

A new role

It is always possible to ask the question 'What is local government for?' To the proponents of municipal socialism a major part of the answer would have involved municipal enterprise and municipal trading. In the era of municipal labourism the emphasis would have shifted towards service provision in fields such as housing, education, social services and planning. In the case of local socialism part of the answer would focus on the role of the council as a resource for political campaigning. Thus the terms of reference of Sheffield's new Employment Department required it to be involved 'not simply in providing services itself but also in acting as a resource for groups and organisations outside the Town Hall' (Bye and Beattie, 1982, p. 8). The concept of the town hall as a machine for service delivery was to be supplemented, though not supplanted, by the notion of using it as a political base from which to campaign within the community on a wide variety of issues, not all of which would necessarily be confined to matters over which the council had any statutory powers.

In some ways this approach was little more than a development of a point made in the Bains report on local authority management structure in 1972:

Local government is not, in our view, limited to the narrow provision of a series of services to the local community . . . It has within its purview the overall economic, cultural and physical well-being of that community . . . (para. 2.10)

However the left's concerns were political rather than managerial and reflected a refusal to allow politics to become compartmentalized by accidents of organization or structure or to allow their own activism to be confined to some local government ghetto. 'If somebody who's asked me to speak on Ireland half a dozen times in the last ten years comes to me after the [GLC] election and says, will you say so and so, I'm not going to behave differently' (Ken Livingstone, in Carvel, 1984, p. 105). It was not however merely a matter of individual behaviour: the whole point of the left's recognition that the local state might provide some 'space' for political activism would have been lost unless they were to take the fullest advantage of it through their local authorities.

Many of the new issues referred to in the previous section have provided the substance of local authority campaigns, for greater police accountability, for meeting women's needs and against racism. Women's committees for example have campaigned both within and without their local authority for job-sharing, for safety in the streets, for improved childcare, for more women to sign on for unemployment benefit and against sexual harassment and sexist advertisements. Such campaigns present local authorities with what are often new involvements in liaison and co-operation with pressure groups, in programmes of conferences and meetings, and in large scale exercises in publicity and public relations. These involvements have sometimes, by virtue of their novelty, entailed the setting up of new campaign units and the taking on of new staff with the connections, commitment and talent appropriate to particular campaigns. Petitions, periodicals, pamphlets, leaflets, information kits, lapel-stickers, posters, postcards, badges, car-stickers, marches, demonstrations, exhibitions, open days, concerts, all of these devices have been employed by authorities concerned with changing local opinion, or supporting local demands, on various issues.

For local authorities whose previous attempts to reach the people may have been little more than the rent collector, the rate demand and the voting registration form such activities are clearly a radical new departure. Paradoxically enough the Conservative government's attempts to abolish the metropolitan counties and the GLC and to introduce rate-capping provided an especially useful set of issues on which left-wing councils could bridge any gaps which might have existed between themselves or their more prosaic predecessors and the public at large. The campaign to save the GLC for example enabled the leadership at County Hall to address itself directly to a wide range of directly affected groups – art lovers, the disabled, conservationists, the elderly – and to preach the virtues of public sector activity and local democracy. The parallel staging of partly recreational and partly propagandist 'events' at the Jubilee Gardens, at County Hall and at the Royal Festival Hall also made for easier access to people who otherwise might never have knowingly come into contact with the GLC. As well as turning public opinion in its favour on the issue of local democracy the campaign also enabled the GLC to present a 'south bank socialism' with a human face.

Using the local authority as a political resource and as a base from which to move out into a wider political arena did not only mean campaigning by the council itself. It also involved facilitating the activities of various groups in the community whose activity or advocacy supplemented the work of the local authority. At one level this could mean little more than giving such groups access to information, to printing or reprographic facilities or to rooms for meetings. But it could also mean financial assistance in the form of grants. This particular form of assistance became one which soon attracted much comment in the media, with John Vincent complaining in *The Times* (9 March 1983) that 'the GLC's main function these days is to pay people to re-elect it' and a *Guardian* editorial (19 September 1984) regretting 'the use of GLC patronage . . . in the form of money for sympathetic groups'.

The GLC's grants programme, although foreshadowed in the 1981 Labour manifesto, was not originally conceived on its eventual scale of £42 million allocated for 1983/4 and £47 million for 1984/5. John

McDonnell, the first chair of the then grants panel in 1981 reported that 'within three months each constituency member was realising that the political returns were absolutely enormous', not perhaps in influencing entire constituencies but in enabling a Labour GLC to 'establish our credentials within certain communities' (quoted in Carvel, 1984, p. 211). In a report to the council on 22 May 1984 McDonnell identified the purpose of grant support as being to 'support voluntary and community organisations for the services they provide, for their contributions to more democratic and open government and as a way of encouraging mutual aid and enriching community life'. There was also a 'general strategy of raising the awareness and expectations of less privileged groups'. Within the overall grant funding of the GLC, including that from the main service committees as well as from the grants sub-committee, grants towards arts and recreation took the largest portion of the total in 1983/4, some 20 per cent. Other categories included women's groups with 13 per cent, training schemes with 11 per cent, employment with 11 per cent, and ethnic minorities with just under 5 per cent.

In Camden in the same year the distribution of grants, on the basis of slightly different categories, was as follows: advice/housing/health and social care, 41·6 per cent; recreation, 30·8 per cent; community development, 27·6 per cent; women's interests, 9·0 per cent; race relations, 8·9 per cent (Raine and Webster, 1984, p. 49). Within each of such categories there are clearly a very wide range of groups being funded, over a thousand in the case of the GLC. As one Conservative Home Office minister, David Waddington, has acknowledged (*Voluntary Action*, June 1984), most of the bodies funded by the GLC have been 'sensible', with the 'bizarre' ones accounting for only 1·8 per cent of the total grant-giving. In fact, despite occasional rather quaint seeming grants (e.g. Islington's £1,000 to the Society for Neutering Islington's Pussies for 1983/4) it is not they which in themselves pose the major problem. Indeed one survey (Raine and Webster, 1984) suggested that smaller and newer (and thus more exotic?) groups were at a disadvantage in the 'group funding market' compared with the larger and longer established organizations. These latter bodies were more likely to have experienced staff who could present a more effective case to a local authority with whose ways they were already quite familiar. From the councillor's angle too there can be problems simply in making judgements on competing claims – Islington's Race Relations Committee was faced with a pile of grant applications and accompanying reports an inch thick at one of its 1983 meetings. As finance gets tighter but knowledge of the existence of grants gets greater such allocation problems clearly become more acute: the GLC estimated that its grants sub-committee would be able to fund only about 16 per cent of the nearly 500 new applications for grant for 1984/5. In such circumstances exercising the politics of patronage becomes an extremely difficult, and also an extremely delicate, task.

New relationships

Hill (1972, p. 211) has commented that 'ideological politics puts great strains upon administrators' not least because it raises the question of 'the ability of highly trained public servants to devote themselves wholeheartedly to the service of a particular party without at the same time compromising themselves'. For some local government officers in left Labour councils the taking on of new issues and new roles by their authority has probably been less problematic than some of the new relationships which have emerged, or been deliberately created, between officers, politicians and political party.

As we have seen many left-wing councillors have been less than impressed with the traditional ways of conducting local authority business. Moreover their disenchantment has embraced not merely the performance of their own predecessors as councillors but also that of local government officers. They have often been particularly receptive to the critiques which developed in the 1970s of professionalism, critiques whose acceptance had considerable implications for a local government service organized very firmly on professionally based departments.

The major elements of these critiques have been summarized by Wilding (1981, p. 17):

> Professional advice gains credibility because of its supposed scientific nature but that is open to question. The paternalism of professional activity is attacked as leading to the neglect of clients' rights and to their disablement. The political neutrality of the professions is unmasked as fundamental conservatism. Accountability to the professional peer group is challenged as an excuse for avoiding genuine accountability.

Criticisms such as these commended themselves to a number of individuals within certain of the local government professions and some of these radicalized professionals, particularly from town planning and social work, have formed one of the constituent parts of the new urban left. Acceptance of such criticisms had certain implications for the way local authorities might function. In particular it encouraged a move away from the traditional practice of committee meetings at which councillors were presented with reports which were anonymously authored, nominally the work of the relevant chief officer, and ostensibly the expression of a collective departmental view of what was the correct professional solution to any given problem.

In place of such practices left-wing authorities began to erode the previous division of labour between officials and politicians. Thus at the GLC 'councillors have begun to break these barriers down by drafting reports and carrying out research with the officers' (*Capital and Class*, 1982, p. 130) while officers themselves were encouraged to produce reports expressing their own views rather than to submerge them in the traditional 'concurrent report' presenting a collective departmental wisdom. In some cases councillors themselves, especially those occupying committee chairs, have presented their own reports and recommendations to their committees rather than rely on reports from officers.

Some of the concerns of the left did not in any case lie within the remit of any of the established professions and in these instances new forms of working were seen as particularly appropriate. In Sheffield the subject of employment was a case in point:

> The exploratory and innovative nature of the jobs to be done by the Employment Department means that a flexible project-style or organisation may be more effective than the traditional pyramid-structure developed to manage established services . . . This kind of less hierarchical, more collective inter-disciplinary project work is familiar in many research and development situations in industry and in action-research projects. (Bye and Beattie, 1982, p. 9)

Such a method of working would in any case already have been familiar to many of the left for it has similarities to that style of operation known as 'networking', with its reliance on ad hoc networks of conferences, workshops and working groups forming and re-forming in response to the needs of the moment, and which has become common amongst contemporary socialists. It is precisely through such rather informal and ad hoc mechanisms that many of the ideas of local socialism have been disseminated on the left in recent years: similar mechanisms have of course developed in fields such as teaching, lecturing, research and community work which have provided the background of many new left activists. Their adoption, or adaptation, for the purposes of policy-making in left-wing local authorities is therefore hardly surprising. Such practices can however be an unwelcome innovation for some senior officers who identify a threat to their own positions or to their departments in the new patterns of working or in the creation of new working groups, strategy groups, policy groups, ethnic minority units, police committee support units, women's units, etc.

It is not however the scale of these innovations that has worried the more conventional officers; in fact many of the new units set up have been very small in size. Indeed it might be argued that their small size and their location outside, or as appendages, of the mainstream departmental structure could make it very easy for established senior officers to shunt them aside and marginalize both them and the issues they were set up to address. What has caused such officers disquiet has been the feeling that though they may well be small in size they may be great in political influence, with those appointed to them being well connected to the political networks of the left in general and of the local majority Labour group in particular. Their fear has been of politics 'spilling over' from being (properly) the concern of elected members to being (improperly) the concern of appointed officers; they fear, perhaps resent, what one chief officer described as 'the officer who thinks he's a member' and whose position is seen as being basically that of political appointment.

The making of such appointments has been argued for quite explicitly by a number of leading figures within local socialism. David Blunkett (1981b, p. 102) felt that

> the people who work for local authorities have got to be committed to a new type of politics. They are not expected to be members of the Labour Party but they should have a commitment, not to an isolated individual but to the community itself. These workers should be able to see that they are part of community action, that they are part of the political education, with a small 'p'.

Rather more explicitly Derek Hatton, from Liverpool, felt that 'we'd want to make sure that . . . those who are employed to manage and carry out the policies which we decide are those who are in general sympathy with those policies' (*Liverpool Echo*, 10 December 1981), while Jim Gillman, chair of Greenwich's Personnel and Industrial Relations Committee, welcomed job applicants 'who are sympathetic to the socialist cause and the aims of this council – that is for the creation and furtherance of a socialist society' (*Standard*, 11 November 1982). In some instances the very nature of some of the jobs was almost bound to invite applications from those with political involvements. Positions in women's and ethnic minorities' units for example were clearly likely to attract applicants whose knowledge and experience were matched by personal involvement with the women's movement or black community groups. Economic policy and employment were fields which attracted job applicants with previous commitments in such fields as local community groups and trades unions.

There is of course a distinction to be made between these appointments and those of political advisers in the form of assistants and researchers appointed to serve party groups, committee chairs and council leaders. The creation of these latter posts pre-dates the emergence of the new urban left, with Nottinghamshire and the GLC for example doing so in 1973/4: ten years later the Labour group at the GLC had some forty people providing various forms of support and assistance. A combination of elected members, political advisers and political appointees could clearly be seen as providing a counterbalance to any tendency towards obstructionism or inertia on the part of the established bureaucracy. It did however entail the possibility of a certain confusion of roles amongst the three groups of people each of whom might see themselves, or be seen by others, as the authorized conveyors of political messages, and sometimes political decisions, in their dealings with professional officers or with groups in the community.

A further possibility of confusion of role, or of allegiance, arose in the case of those officers – whether 'political' or professional – who were also serving simultaneously as councillors in another authority. The two-tier system of local government which replaced the county boroughs in the metropolitan counties in 1974, had facilitated the emergence of such councillors, though even without it it would still have been possible to serve, say, in one district as an employee and in a neighbouring district as a councillor. The practice was also given an impetus by the desire of radicalized professionals to give expression to those political elements of their work which they felt were stifled within the conventional forms of local authority employment. The extent of this practice is not yet adequately investigated. However, one small scale survey in 1982 found that one in five of left Labour councillors who were in employment worked in local government (Lipsey, 1982) while another investigation in the same year of five inner London boroughs plus the GLC (Walker, 1983) found that education, local government and voluntary organizations (often council-funded) accounted for the jobs of 41 per cent of those who were economically active. The possible confusions to which this might give rise were instanced by one chief officer whose committee chair was also political adviser to the chair of the equivalent committee in a nearby authority. At meetings between the two authorities it was not always clear to the chief officer which of his two roles the chair/political adviser was performing. Framing the problem in this way of course presupposes that questions of institutional loyalty, in this instance to a particular local authority, are or should be of major importance. Yet this proposition would not be regarded as self-evident amongst the new urban left. They see their own local authority as important only in so far as it provides a framework, or a base, within or from which they can translate socialism into practice on the ground. An individual council is thus a means to an ideological end, not an end in itself.

Such a view of local government might not commend itself to conventional local government officers who in the course of a career may reckon to see politicians and political trends come and go and for whom professional, departmental and local authority loyalties may be seen as more important and more enduring frames of reference. It is of course against this same institution-bound inertia, as they see it, that left-wing councillors feel compelled to struggle. In the course of their struggle against the 'town hall embrace' a crucial role is allotted to the local Labour party outside the council.

Ever since the 1930s the Labour Party's rules have always given local party organizations the right to determine what policies shall be offered to the voters at local elections. Between elections however decisions on policy matters became the prerogative of Labour groups. It was not until quite recently however that local parties began to devote serious attention to policy formulation for local elections, usually contenting themselves with rather bland but well-intentioned generalizations or slogans. However from the mid-1970s onwards more detailed manifestos began to appear for the elections to some of the larger authorities. The Labour manifesto for the 1981 GLC elections was prepared over a two-year period by some two hundred people in six working parties, whose efforts culminated in a document 157 pages long. Having prepared such detailed proposals many activists were not prepared, once the elections were over, simply to hand the manifesto to elected Labour councillors and let them get on with the task of implementation. They saw themselves as not only the creators of the manifesto but also as its 'guardians', whose protection and advocacy it might need if Labour councillors came under pressure from officers to dilute or discard certain proposals.

For it should not be imagined that new left councillors have been exempt from some of the suspicions with which left-wing activists had often regarded their more right-wing predecessors. Within one year of their election to office in 1981 for example the Labour ILEA and GLC were subject to considerable criticism over their performance in certain quarters. They were thought to have suffered major reverses on bus fares, school meals, rents and the transfer of housing estates to the boroughs. One critic declared that 'majority opposition is now the only honourable course for the comrades at County Hall to follow'; another feared the prospect of 'watching a Labour administration, elected on a radical manifesto, having its policies shot to pieces within a year . . . clinging to office by its finger-nails and justifying its surrender with the same weary arguments that any Labour council is better than a Tory/SDP one' (*London Labour Briefing*, April, 1982). Such criticisms receded however as the GLC became a major target of Conservative attack and as its vigorous defence of its existence, if not of its more radical policies, was seen to have made a major impact on public opinion.

In some of the London boroughs however similar criticisms flared up from time to time. Industrial action amongst social workers in Southwark in 1983 produced dissatisfaction over the council's dealings with NALGO; combined with earlier council treatment of squatters it was instanced as an example of 'the unparalleled houdini power of Southwark Council Labour Group to eat its own manifesto'. Further north, in April 1984 the Hackney Labour Parties Borough Conference, composed of the Labour group and the two Hackney constituency party general committees, 'decided to correct some of the mistakes made by the Council leadership over the past two years': it did so by electing a new leadership 'to make sure that Hackney Council carried out the decisions made by the Labour Party in Hackney' since the previous leadership 'could not shake free of its appalling industrial relations nor galvanise support from local people'. Next door a few months later, an Islington councillor resigned from the council, complaining at the council's handling of a dispute with nursery workers, accusing some fellow councillors of having 'broken with the position of their wards and their ward mandates' and wondering whether there might be some 'fundamental political flaws in the attitude of the left to the role of councillors'. What was more the joint meetings of the Islington Labour group and the joint Local Government Committee of the two Islington constituency parties had failed to work as a mechanism of account-ability 'because members of the party didn't turn up' (*London Labour Briefing*, December 1983; May, June and August, 1984).

Islington's Local Government Committee was however far from typical in its apparent apathy towards relations with its Labour group. A very different experience has been that of Lewisham where

a number of important structural changes have occurred including making Group meetings open to all Labour Party members in Lewisham; having 6 LGC reps on the Group Policy Committee, co-opting LGC reps onto various Council committees, having joint LGC/Group meetings once a quarter; receiving regular written and verbal reports from every Council Committee Chair. It has also been recently agreed that the LGC reps will attend the Group AGM with full voting rights in the election of all the Committee Chairs, Group Officers and the Leader and Deputy Leader. (*London Labour Briefing*, February 1984)

At the Lewisham Labour group AGM in May 1984 thirty-three Local Government Committee members attended along with thirty-seven councillors: they elected a new leader, Ron Stockbridge, who regarded himself as having been 'elected more by the Party than by

the Group' (*London Labour Briefing*, June 1984) and who thereafter
was faced by local party pressure to operate a policy of mass
resignations of Labour councillors in the autumn to be followed by
by-elections on a platform of 'no cuts, no rent rises, no rate rises'.
Such a policy however did not commend itself to the Labour group
and was not carried out, to the disquiet of some activists.

To some observers it would appear ironic that left-wing Labour
councils should find themselves under such pressures from their own
left-wing activists; even more so that they should fall into conflict
with local trades unions, not only in Islington and Southwark, but
also in Lambeth and Haringey. Some councils have made particular
efforts to involve their unions in decision-making. In Sheffield

> the council's own workforce – thirty thousand strong – meets
> regularly in worktime – department by department, with
> councillors and trade union spokesmen – and each employee
> receives bulletins explaining the latest position. (Blunkett, 1981a)

Liverpool has gone so far as to co-opt twelve members of the Joint
Shop Stewards Executive Committee as non-voting advisory
representatives on its Personnel Committee and has also agreed that
the unions should be represented on all interviewing panels for
vacancies and promotions.

Despite such initiatives, difficulties can still arise. In its
confrontation with the government over its budget for 1984/5, for
example, Liverpool found it could not rely on support from the
National Union of Teachers (NUT) or the National Union of Public
Employees (NUPE), though the white collar National and Local
Government Officers Association (NALGO) and the major manual
workers union the General Municipal, Boilermakers and Allied
Trade Union (GMBATU) did back the council's strategy. In London
some of the initiatives of decentralizing services have met with
suspicion and hostility from certain unions, a problem which had
also occurred earlier in the case of Walsall. Such problems can
sometimes reflect differences between the union leadership and the
rank and file. Thus Ken Livingstone (1984, p. 270) discovered that
although 'the leadership of NALGO in London is very much in line
with radical socialist policies, it's completely out of sympathy with
the bulk of its members' who had rather different priorities of their
own. On other occasions though, as in the case of the Islington
nursery workers, some trades unionists and party activists have been
in alliance against the council leadership, who have been cast in the
roles of socialist backsliders.

Such conflicts, whatever the particular issues at their centre, are
not always mere differences of opinion about how to handle a

particular local problem. They are sometimes bound up with the manoeuvrings of particular left-wing groups inside and outside the Labour Party, for example the *Socialist Organiser* group on the inside and the SWP on the outside, the latter being particularly influential in certain branches of NALGO. In such instances they are a manifestation of the strategy of 'outflanking from the left' in the hope of thereby pushing the Labour Party into taking positions which imply outright confrontation with the present social and political system.

The emergence of such divisions amongst councillors, party activists and trades unionists might well cause surprise to those who see the left as a monolithic entity. In particular it might well surprise those who interpret the new urban left as some form of new tightly-knit political machine bent on exploiting the new issues, the new roles and the new relationships it has developed as devices for seizing and retaining political power.

A new machine?

To describe a group of politicians and their supporters as constituting a machine may not be to say anything other than that they organize themselves specifically, and perhaps effectively, for the purpose of gaining and retaining power. In the terms of such a broad definition the advance of the left in local government, and indeed in the Labour Party at large, might well be seen as the advance of a machine. *London Labour Briefing*'s Target '82 campaign to secure the adoption of left-wing candidates and left-wing policies for the London borough elections and the earlier campaign for similar purposes in respect of the GLC could both be interpreted as carefully organized operations complete with card-indexes, pre-meetings and having the right people in the right place at the right time. In fact such an interpretation is truer in the case of the GLC than of the London boroughs, where the left's organization was sometimes patchy and where the patterns of possible candidacies could be confused by the debates within some left factions about whether to put pressure on an elected Labour council from within or from without. However, whatever the nature of the campaigns which brought the left to power, there have been those who have suggested that once in power. they have been intent on creating a machine which will ensure their retention of that power, a machine moreover which draws not merely on the resources of the party but on public funds as well.

Thus Richard Brew, Conservative leader on the GLC during 1982/3, saw the GLC's grant-funding programme as an attempt at 'hard-headed manipulation' of the electorate in the hope that grants would produce votes in return. By providing financial aid, and thereby also providing some jobs to particular groups and individual activists, the GLC was creating 'a system of winning power with methods not seen in this country since the eighteenth century' (quoted in Carvel, 1984, pp. 208 and 210). In *The Times* (9 September 1983) John Vincent echoed this refrain, suggesting that some might conclude

> that London now being more than ever a melting pot, a half-foreign city, Mr Livingstone's Walpolian system of client groups and patronage is actually the right way to run it.

Indeed, he went on, in ironical vein,

> Tammany Hall, some now argue was not corrupt: perish the thought, it served old-style New York well by performing what is genteely called an integrative function. (Or in other words it gave every Irishman a job as a cop.)

The Tammany Hall reference was taken up later by the Islington SDP councillor David Hyams who used the council's own *Islington Focus* (April 1984) to complain at the possible influence of non-elected Labour activists at meetings of the Labour group with the local party's Local Government Committee: 'Secret discussions of public matters and private attempts to influence decision making are characteristic of Tammany Hall politics'. In the same borough in 1983 a series of public meetings on proposals to create decentralized neighbourhood offices had raised two queries, among many others, from those attending: 'Will these offices be used generally to help local people and not as a political machine?' and 'Is it just another scheme for more "jobs for the boys"?' The latter point also worried some members of the *Beyond the Fragments* network whose *Bulletin* (Winter 1982–3) expressed the fear that in appointing socialists to key posts 'Progressive Labour Councils . . . end up either appointing the wrong people, or appointing the right people and turning them into members of a privileged elite'.

At first sight there do appear to be many similarities between the operations of the new urban left and the classic political machines of urban America in the late nineteenth and early twentieth centuries. The latter focused on local government, though they also used it as a base from which to try and influence higher levels of politics; they were concerned to build a coalition of lower-class voters including particularly the various ethnic minority groups; they provided financial and other aid for those groups to whom they looked for support; they made political appointments to official positions in the local authority; and they gave the local party organization a key role in decision-making. A major attraction which they possessed for their clientele was that they offered a 'contrast to the professional techniques of the welfare worker which . . . typically represent[ed] in the mind of the recipient the cold, bureaucratic dispensation of limited aid' (Merton, 1968, p. 128).

The machine did of course have its opponents. It was vigorously attacked in the local press and it drew vocal opposition from the professional and commercial classes. The latter indeed sought to offer an alternative form of urban politics, a more 'businesslike' and managerial style of local government. While employing the language of democratic propriety and accountability, the anti-machine reformers also pressed the claims of 'efficiency, system, orderliness, budgets, economy, saving . . . [and] sought to re-model municipal government in terms of the great impersonality of corporate enterprise' (Shannon, 1940, p. 168).

These characteristics, both of the classic American machines and of their 'reforming' opponents, do seem to convey a foretaste of certain features now encountered amongst the new urban left and their Thatcherite enemies. Yet tempting or intriguing historical parallels can easily be carried too far. For one thing the American machine was a phenomenon which endured for several decades; the new urban left has a history of but a few years and the trajectory of its future development remains unknown. Moreover it is not clear whether the left have the organizational staying power which enabled the machine to endure over so many years. Those who joined the Labour Party in the early 1960s, left it in the late 1960s, moved into community action or single issue politics or left sectarianism, then rejoined Labour in the late 1970s – may they not yet move on again if the hopes or expectations which they have placed in local socialism are not fulfilled?

It is in any case the nature of those hopes and expectations which differentiate the new urban left most clearly from the old machine politics. In practice the latter took quite a variety of forms but its different manifestations had one common denominator, namely that of being 'a non-ideological electoral organisation, depending heavily on lower-class votes' (Lineberry and Sharkansky, 1978, p. 119). The new urban left may well address itself primarily to lower-class voters, and it may or may not try, like any electoral organization, to establish 'credentials within certain communities' in John McDonnell's words. But one thing is quite clear – it is not 'non-ideological'. Martin Lomasney, the Democratic Party boss of Boston's West End, used to claim that his machine offered 'help you understand, none of your law and your justice but help' (quoted in Kaplan, 1975, p. 65). The purpose of local socialism is not merely the practical one of offering help to those in need: it is also the ideological one of promoting radical social change through political action at the grass roots.

4   New Strategies for Socialism

> To place in the hands of the local community a resource which they can exploit for the purposes of influencing policy, exploring new ideas and furthering control over their own lives. (The aims of neighbourhood offices as set out in *Haul to Democracy*, the Walsall Labour Manifesto, 1980)

If the ambition to secure radical change through grass-roots politics is to be more than a vague aspiration it clearly has to be translated into some specific courses of action. If there is to be a local road to socialism then the elements of the journey need to be identified.

One possible element lies simply in the general power of example, with 'the local state used as an example of what we could do as a Socialist government at national level' (Blunkett, 1981b, p. 102). While it would clearly be 'too romantic a vision to conjure up a picture of socialist republics operating on a local scale in an otherwise non-socialist environment' it might be possible for 'progressive local authorities [to] help to set the atmosphere in which central government can be changed' (Leeson, 1981, p. 19). Historically there has certainly been a long tradition of pace-setting local authorities charting courses for others to follow. Leeds, for example, was something of a 'Mecca' for housing reformers in the 1930s and became a model of Conservative frugality in the 1970s. More recently Walsall's experiment with decentralized neighbourhood offices has been a subject of great interest to Labour councillors from other authorities, who have tried to discover what lessons it may have to teach. Local models of socialism then, may have a part to play by developing the repertoire of policies and procedures available to like-minded councils and by challenging the accepted wisdom as to what is desirable or possible.

However the chances are that much of the exchange of ideas and experiences implied by such local models will take place largely amongst those politicians and other activists who are already connected into the political networks of the left. If the mass of ordinary people are to travel along the local road to socialism then additional strategies will be required. In the literature and practice of local socialism two particular strategies stand out quite clearly, namely those of decentralization and mobilization.

Decentralization

There is of course a long, and comparatively neglected, tradition of decentralist socialism not only in Britain but in Europe. What has been described as 'self-governing socialism' (Horvat *et al.*, 1975) has been advocated in a variety of forms by socialists such as G. D. H. Cole and William Morris, Proudhon and Kropotkin and, as we have seen, by some of the early municipal socialists. A periodic enthusiasm for decentralist ideas is not however confined solely to the political left. There are other ideologies which have their decentralist versions and from time to time it seems as if there is a decentralist light shining through all parts of the political spectrum.

Thus it was for example that writing on the eve of the First World War, Ernest Barker observed that 'a certain tendency to discredit the State [was] now abroad' in all quarters, with syndicalism and guild socialism on the left being matched by Belloc's distributivism on the right and with nationalism and religion finding anti-statist expression in demands for Home Rule and Church disestablishment. On the left, 'collectivism of the Fabian order was the dominant form of Socialism in England till within the last three or four years', but in 1914 'the newest Socialism has abandoned the paths of a unitary collectivism managed from a single centre'. There had been a 'struggle with the "administrative" Socialism of the Fabian school and . . . [a] revolt against its definite recognition of the State as the organ of Socialism . . . [since] the governing class under State-Socialism becomes a bureaucracy, regimenting and controlling the life of the citizen'. In place of state socialism, the possibilities of syndicalism and of guild socialism had begun to excite the imaginations of socialists (Barker, 1963 edn, pp. 197–8 and 222).

The outbreak of anti-statism which Barker observed in 1914 was short-lived. The use of the machinery of government to mobilize the nation for total war suddenly seemed to re-establish the credentials of the state as a potential force for good, particularly on the political left. In the early months of the war the Labour Party's *Daily Citizen* celebrated the fact that

> Thus in the hour of its supreme need does the nation turn to the collectivist experiments urged for so many years by the Labour movement. And the experiments are not found wanting. They are absolutely and brilliantly vindicated . . . will it not be sound policy to continue the experiment during what we hope will be the long years of unbroken peace? (Quoted in Marwick, 1967, p. 173)

Similarly Sidney Webb remarked that 'we have had, during the war, a great deal of control of capital . . . *can we afford to relinquish that control when peace comes?'* (Webb, 1917, p. 29, emphasis in original). The utility of the state as a means of controlling the economy became increasingly widely accepted within the Labour Party as the war progressed and the 1918 policy statement *Labour and the New Social Order* gave clear expression to the belief that the state's powers should thereafter be used during the period of postwar reconstruction and afterwards.

The relevance of recalling Ernest Barker's celebration of what turned out to be a rather short-lived flowering of a widespread anti-statism is that it reminds us of two things. The first is that what appears at any one time to be the great enthusiasm of the moment may not necessarily prove to be the wave of the future. The second is that the tendency to see the state as a major part either of the solution or of the problem of society's ills need not be confined to any one wing of politics. In 1914 Barker (p. 107) felt able to assert that in the retreat from the state, whether led from the right or the left, 'the idea of the guild ... is the idea of the hour'. Seventy years later another commentator had a similar perception, namely that 'we are all decentralisers now' (Wright, 1984, p. 1). Wright's observation echoes that of an American political scientist who had earlier hailed decentralization as 'one of the great, resonant themes of contemporary politics' (Polsby, 1979, p. 1). Decentralization may of course take many forms and be the product of a variety of inspirations. In the first half of the 1980s local socialism was not the only instance of decentralist ideas in Britain and its own pre-occupations begin to stand out all the more clearly when it is contrasted with some of the decentralisms being canvassed in other quarters.

Conservative 'ratepayer democracy'

Traditionally the Conservative Party saw itself as the sworn opponent of centralization, which it identified with socialism, and it therefore claimed a role as the champion of local government. Thus in 1948 the party's conference resolved:

> That this Conference opposes the Socialist Government's policy of centralisation of control and the general tendency to take away the functions of the Local Authorities, and place them in the hands of non-elected bodies ...

In the following year the party issued an official statement of party policy which began with the assertion that

> The governing principle of Conservative and Unionist policy on Local Government, is that Local Government should be Local,

and that it should be Government ... Merely to pass on orders from the central authorities ... is not Local Government.

The Conservative defence of local government as a bulwark against centralization was encapsulated in the choice of Disraeli's warning that 'centralisation is the death-blow of public freedom' as the motto with which to adorn the cover of the party's journal *The Councillor* between 1948 and 1953. In more recent times the party's 1970 general election manifesto had complained that 'under Labour there has been too much government interference in the day-to-day workings of ... local government' and had pledged that since 'the independence of local authorities has been seriously eroded by Labour Ministers ... we will redress the balance and increase the independence of local authorities'. In February 1974 however the manifesto merely recorded that 'local government services have continued to expand during our term of office' and that the government had increased its 'help to the ratepayers to meet the cost of that expansion'.

In October 1974 there came a clear change of tone. In a separate section of the manifesto titled 'People and Rates' it was asserted that

Local authority expenditure has been growing faster than the economy as a whole ... the burden on the domestic ratepayer has risen sharply ... within the normal lifetime of a Parliament we shall abolish the domestic rating system and replace it by taxes more broadly based and related to people's ability to pay.

The commitment to abolish the rating system had arisen from the recommendations of a Conservative working group on local government finance set up by Margaret Thatcher during her time as front-bench environment spokesman between the two elections of 1974. There were those who feared it might prove to be something of an albatross around the party's neck, a pledge which could not be fulfilled and it was 'reluctantly' omitted from the 1979 manifesto (Butler and Kavanagh, 1980, p. 158). In 1983 however the party manifesto contemplated government action against excessive rate increases by high-spending councils and the outright abolition of the GLC and the six metropolitan county councils.

In effect the decade before 1983 saw the Conservative Party gradually moving away from its traditional posture as the defender of local government against centralization to a new posture as the defender of the ratepayer against local government. The new posture was put quite clearly by the then Secretary of State for the Environment, Michael Heseltine, at the annual meeting of the Association of County Councils in July 1979:

I have to make it clear to you that as sponsoring minister for local
government I am not only the sponsoring minister for the rate
spenders and the rate collectors but in the last resort for the
ratepayers as well.

In its new role the government felt it necessary to intervene actively
on the side of the ratepayer against local government by means of
central government initiatives such as the new block grant system,
the abortive proposal for rates referendums, rate-capping, com-
pulsory consultation with commercial and industrial ratepayers and
abolition of the GLC and metropolitan counties. Much of the
rhetoric used in defence of such initiatives still contained echoes of
decentralist ideas, a conjunction which some Conservatives found
rather confusing. Thus Sir Horace Cutler, then Conservative leader
of the GLC, protested over the proposals for block grant at his party's
1980 local government conference: 'We are trying to decentralise . . .
in an effort to get the state off of the backs of the people and yet here
we have a Bill seeking to enshrine the principles of centralist control'.
Sir Horace saw decentralization in terms of developing power to
lower levels of government, and since he believed the Thatcher
government to be 'committed . . . to encouraging local autonomy' he
was thus much agitated at the idea of that same government devising
new forms of central control over local authorities. In fact the
government was not particularly concerned with decentralization
from central government to local government; its chief enthusiasm
was for decentralization from all levels of government to the
individual.

Moreover the individual who was to benefit from this new wave of
decentralization was not merely the individual as citizen, it was also
the individual as economic man. Hence the concern that local
authorities should be held more accountable not merely to the
citizens as voters but also to commercial and industrial ratepayers
who were seen as being in some way 'unrepresented' through the
normal processes of democratic elections. Thus in the context of
local government, Thatcherite decentralization took not the
traditional Conservative form of defending the existing institutions of
local democracy but that of embracing a new 'ratepayer democracy'.
Local government itself was seen as being as much in need of a rolling
back of its frontiers as was central government, in order that
economic individualism might have greater room for action. Ratepayer democracy not only implied less money for local government.
It also implied less local government, with fewer services to provide
since some of them could be handed over to the private sector to the
supposed benefit of consumers and ratepayers alike.

In its attacks on local government bureaucracy and its constituent professions Thatcherism was every bit as scathing as the left. Heseltine complained to the 1980 Conservative local government conference about a 'bureaucratic machine' which had 'a mind and a will of its own'; Michael Forsyth (1981), a keen advocate of privatization of local services, wrote dismissively of local government being 'top heavy with unnecessary layers of bureaucracy' and of its 'impersonal, sneering professionals'. Left and right thus identified some similar symptoms of local government's malaise: but they differed profoundly in their diagnoses and in their preferred remedies.

Liberal community politics

Local socialism and ratepayer democracy are not the only formulae on offer to those seeking an alternative to conventional patterns of local government and politics. In 1980 the Liberal Party's annual assembly passed the following resolution:

> In determining the organisational strategy to achieve Liberal aims, this Assembly endorses the following objectives as of prime importance:
>
> (1)   a dual approach to politics, working both inside and outside the institutions of the political establishment;
> (2)   a primary strategic emphasis on community politics; our role as political activists is to help people in communities to organise to take and use power, to use our political skills to redress grievances and to represent people at all levels of the political structure.

The 'primary strategic emphasis on community politics' became the distinctive feature of Liberal politics after 1970, with the party placing much emphasis on local government activity and claiming a distinctive 'bottom up' view of local government emphasizing diversity and decentralization. As a strategy of political advance it proved to have its uses, as the growing number of Liberal councillors after 1970 indicated. However it was also seen by some of its adherents as a new form of libertarian politics which could provide an alternative to the postwar welfare state consensus and as such its emergence pre-dated the local socialism of the left.

The local socialism of the left certainly invites comparison with the community politics of the Liberals since both stress the virtues of decentralization and grass-roots activism. The two forms of politics clearly seem to echo one another in certain respects. For example, both are concerned with building up political support, albeit in rather differing ways. Thus the 'advice centres, community newsletters, petitions, action groups and grumble sheets' (Mole, 1983, p. 260) of community politics have 'become largely associated in Liberal minds with the fighting and winning of Council seats' (Bingham, 1981, p. 22). For the left, though, the process of building support is not so much a question of doorstep electioneering as of building a 'new coalition' embracing such groups as 'the trade unions, ethnic minority organisations, women's movement, tenants' and residents' associations' who have previously been overlooked in 'the confines of Council Chamber politics' (*London Labour Briefing*, June 1982).

In neither case, however, is the process of building political support seen as an end in itself. Thus one of the theorists of Liberal community politics argues that it 'is not and never has been a means of winning elections . . . [but] is the process by which a community articulates its objectives and takes measures to determine its own future': the Liberal role is 'to act as the catalyst in the process' (Greaves, 1980, pp. 15 and 17). Meadowcroft (1982a, p. 3) talks of 'the task of raising the political consciousness of the people . . . It is only thus that the latent compassion and neighbourliness can be realised.' In the case of local socialism there is a similar concern with 'not paternalistically doing things for people but throwing our weight behind them . . . to do what they want to do in their way in their community' (Blunkett, 1981b, p. 102). As for raising consciousness, this, too, is an aspiration of local socialism, but it manifests itself in the more specific terms of the 'development of socialist conscious- ness' (Leeson, 1981, p. 16) and of 'shifting the general climate of opinion to the left' (Clarke and Griffiths, 1982, p. 9).

The building of political support and the raising of popular consciousness thus imply rather different things to community politics and to local socialism. The differences confirm McDonnell's (1983, p. 4) assertion that 'Decentralization is politically neutral . . . What is crucial is the form of decentralization and the political philosophy behind it.' In the case of community politics its exponents are clear that it is linked to 'the traditional Liberal belief in the value of the individual . . . powerless in the face of big bureaucracy' (Blackmore, 1982, p. 17) and is 'oriented to the maximum individual freedom within the greatest possible degree of local autonomy, consistent with representative democracy' (Mole, 1980, p. 19). For the left the aim is to make a reality of 'ideas which reflect libertarian, democratic socialist values in a community setting' (Blunkett and Green, 1983, p. 28) and 'to create an authentic form of socialism rooted, not in hierarchical structures, but directly in the people' (Hain, 1980b, p. 6).

Differences emerge clearly in the case of the economic context of decentralization. The left argue that 'the Alliance will not be able to decentralise power because it is unwilling to tackle the sources of economic centralisation inherent in capitalism' but will instead promote 'a kind of specious localism without resources ... Decentralisation without redistribution of wealth and resources means that the poor areas will remain poor and the powerless stay powerless' (Labour Co-ordinating Committee, 1982, pp. 2 and 21). To Liberals, however, such an approach means that 'the Labour Left is wedded to the construction of an economic framework into which the individual and the community have to fit. Such a process is inimical to human nature' (Meadowcroft, 1982a, p. 7).

Differences also exist over the concepts of class and community. Meadowcroft (1982b, p. 3) speculates that the Liberals 'have much to offer the "left" on an understanding of community, whilst Labour has much to offer on the perception of class', admits that 'we are weak on class' (1984, p. 16), and suggests (1982a, p. 25) that 'Liberals could admit that they have something to learn about the politics of the workplace if the Labour Left accepted its ignorance on community concepts'. Such an approach is unlikely to find favour on the Labour left where class and community are not accorded equivalent conceptual weight. For the left 'community- and issue- rather than class-based mobilisation' merely provides scope for 'the occupational and cultural advantages' of the 'credential-holding middle-class stratum ... organising their access to benefits from the means of consumption both individual and collective' (Rustin, 1983, p. 27).

Thus local socialism and community politics differ on some basic issues, related to their underlying philosophies: these in turn reflect the left's preoccupation with, and the Liberals' denial of, capitalism and its class categories as the central political problem. There are those on the Liberal side who would see such differences as problems worth discussing rather than as insuperable barriers. Thus Michael Meadowcroft (1984, p. 15) has asked

Why do we not learn from each other, or find some common ground which will defeat the reactionary view which is counter to both ...? Liberals are very weak on trades unionism, because of their tradition, whereas we have a healthier view of ecological perspectives than does the Labour Left.

There is however little sign that the Labour left is much interested in such a venture, nor indeed that it sees community politics as a serious competitor to local socialism. In any case left-wing activists 'don't seem to be interested in what people outside the Labour Party believe in and argue for' (Anderson, 1983). If anything the left have been rather more concerned, and sometimes perplexed, about what might be seen as yet another different form of decentralization, namely voluntary action in the field of welfare provision.

Voluntary action

Relations have been uncertain and uneasy between local socialism and what Ward (1978) has described as 'self-help socialism . . . a self-help, self-organising society'. The latter concept is epitomized by those 'volunteers for socialism' whom Worpole (1981) finds

> in adult education, trade unions, tenants' organisations, youth clubs and playgroups, local history groups and writers' workshops, handicapped organisations, self-organised sports clubs and societies [and] who, a generation ago . . . would have been active in the Labour Party.

Such forms of 'voluntary action' raise a number of issues for local socialism over and above those posed by the left's tradition of regarding voluntary workers as interfering do-gooders in the tradition of Lady Bountiful.

There are a variety of forms of activity within the voluntary sector of welfare provision – informal networks of caring by family and friends; self-help groups; and voluntary organizations, many funded in greater or larger part by state or charitable sources. Such forms of voluntary action have commended themselves to the ideologists of the new right who look forward to replacing public sector workers 'who cost so much money, by those who provide their help free', namely volunteers (Forsyth, 1981). More generally a growth in the voluntary sector would fit in well with the Thatcherite ambitions of reducing the role of the state, cutting back public spending, undermining public sector trades unions and shifting the responsibility for caring on to the local community or the family or in practice, women.

However there is also a tradition of active involvement by the left in certain forms of voluntary action – claimants' unions, community action groups, sections of the Women's Movement, and more recently the support groups created during the miners' strike. Some of these have been defended from the left on a number of grounds: they have developed more direct forms of accountability; they employ more democratic working practices; they offer alternatives to state or market provision; and they help to demystify the claims of professional expertise (Lawrence, 1983). Considerations such as these suggest that voluntary action might be expected to commend itself in some degree to the proponents of local socialism. Certainly some of the supporters of voluntary action, such as Gladstone (1979) and Hadley and Hatch (1981), are credited with having been 'concerned with many of the same issues as feminist and socialist critiques; notably democratisation, decentralisation, [and] non-hierarchical working' (Beresford and Croft, 1984, p. 34).

Nevertheless, such concern, sincere though it is, is not enough to commend itself wholly to the left. Unlike many of the community groups which developed during the era of the CDP, few voluntary groups concern themselves with the structural origins of the problems with which they are trying to deal. They are thus seen by many on the left as at best misguided and at worst irrelevant or even counter-productive in that in their own way they may obscure the real causes of social injustices. Moreover attempts to justify the activities of the voluntary sector, under the aegis of notions of 'welfare pluralism', are seen as hostages to fortune since they articulate arguments about a desirable variety of non-public sector provision which could be used to justify the spread of market-based private sector schemes or of greater demands for home-based care by women.

Thus although voluntary action, in some respects at least, comes far closer to some of the aims of local socialism than does Liberal community politics or Conservative ratepayer democracy it ultimately fails to be wholly acceptable. This is because it is not specifically focused on enabling people to understand the need to defend existing socialist gains, albeit in the imperfect forms of the welfare state, and to formulate new socialist demands in the form of changes in the present structures of power. These aspirations of local socialism require other mechanisms for their realization than those provided by voluntary groups, though some of the latter may have a supporting role to play. One such mechanism may be found by the creation of new decentralized forms of local government within the present pattern of local authorities.

'Going local'

The term 'going local' has become a form of shorthand for the attempts being made by a number of Labour councils to devise workable models of decentralization, following in the wake of Walsall's example between 1980 and 1982. In London a number of Labour boroughs have committed themselves to such a course – Camden, Greenwich, Hackney, Haringey, Islington, Lambeth and Lewisham. Outside London both Manchester and Birmingham – the latter under right-wing Labour leadership – have also agreed to introduce schemes of decentralization of council services.

The case for decentralization has often been presented to the public in fairly modest and prosaic terms. Camden, for example, spoke of 'closer links between councillors, local people and council workers', of avoiding 'unnecessary delays, confusion, mistrust and frayed tempers' and of giving local people 'more say and influence over what happens in their areas' (*Camden's Going Local* leaflet, 1983). In more overtly political terms it has been claimed that decentralization is 'socialism in action at local level' and that 'going local is the fundamental response necessary to meet the devastating challenge to local government from the Tories' (Labour Co-ordinating Committee, 1984, pp. 2 and 7). In this context decentralization is given a key role in winning back the popular support of those who are thought to have become alienated from the Labour Party, from local government and from the welfare state in recent times.

The complexities of implementation have sometimes proved greater than foreseen, and one Labour councillor closely involved came to fear that decentralization might yet prove to be 'a cross between a sacred cow and an albatross'. In any event, there have been considerable variations in the ways the local authorities have approached the subject. These variations have covered such matters as the range of functions to be decentralized (usually housing, sometimes also planning, welfare rights, personal social services, environmental health); the number of local areas around which services might be organized (32 in Walsall, 24 in Islington, 14 in Camden); and the consultation procedures in preparation for the schemes (varying degrees of 'fluidity' or 'firmness' in the proposals put to public meetings). Problems encountered have included resistance, or at least hesitancy, from unions and local government professions; future relations between local area-based offices/committees and the wider service-based council decision-making structure; the costs of the schemes in times of pressure on local authority spending; and the question of the forms of political representation and control in local areas.

Because of such problems the pace of advance has generally proved slower than some would have liked. Thus Islington, which began to decentralize housing repairs in mid-1983, was probably the most well-advanced with its plans, and had hoped to open its first four neighbourhood offices during 1984. However the actual opening date underwent successive postponements into 1985, partly as a result of a NALGO boycott of the first four advertised posts of neighbourhood officers on the grounds that job descriptions had not been agreed. In Hackney an even more fundamental dispute with NALGO meant that after April 1983 the union boycotted all work on decentralization in protest against what it regarded as inadequate assurances on twelve points ranging from guarantees against job losses to adequate training for new duties. There have also been occasional political problems within the Labour Party. Camden's initial proposals for thirteen neighbourhood areas were rejected at a borough Labour Party conference in January 1983 with complaints about a 'top-down reorganisation' and demands that 'the Group should not miss . . . breaking up existing power structures' within the council (*London Labour Briefing*, March 1983).

The delays and complications recounted above have created a very different situation from that which prevailed at Walsall, where decentralization, chiefly of housing services, was pushed through in two years, with the original Housing Department at the town hall being almost wholly dismantled and some 150 of its staff being relocated in 32 neighbourhood offices, along with nearly 80 newly appointed and sympathetically-minded officers who were committed to the success of the venture. This is not to suggest that there were no difficulties – at one point the council leader and the chief executive were not on speaking terms – but rather that there was an insistence on the politicians taking the initiative even at the risk of treading on toes. In any case NALGO in Walsall was weak and badly organized compared with some of the branches in inner London. Moreover the politicians were very conscious of decentralization as being ultimately more than just a matter of better service delivery. In addition to handling rents, lettings, repairs, rebates and benefits advice the neighbourhood offices have also acted as venues for meetings for pensioners, the unemployed, youth groups, and community and tenants' associations thus facilitating the first steps in 'an attempt to use local government as a place for political education where the individual can learn to understand his/her own democratic power – where socialism could flourish' (David, 1983, p. 75).

It is just such an interpretation which runs through an account of the Walsall initiative published by Jeremy Seabrook in 1984. The significance of his account lies not in any pretensions to a rigorous empirical analysis of what has occurred, for the author makes no such claims, but rather in Seabrook's ability to capture very clearly the left-wing aspirations which underlie not merely decentralization in particular but local socialism in general.

The importance of Walsall's neighbourhood experiment in Seabrook's eyes goes beyond the provision of a more responsive and accessible service. He sees in the experiment the possibility of halting 'a certain retreat from community, the faltering, in large sections of the working class, of commitment to collective values, the withdrawing, not of the outer forms, but of the very roots of solidarity itself'. The neighbourhood idea 'aims to build on the resources and abilities that exist in the communities, to act as a focus for people's own strengths . . . It is a question of inspiring confidence where it has been eroded, of reflecting and supporting the values and defences of working-class people which have been under such sustained attack over the years.' In the words of the sub-title of this book this is 'what local politics should be about' (Seabrook, 1984, pp. 3–4 and 71–2).

Since the Conservatives regained control of the council in 1982 Walsall's initiative has had a sense of marking time, and two of the neighbourhood offices have been shut down. None the less Seabrook (1984, p. 128) feels able to record important gains:

> People have been given fresh confidence that they can work for their own neighbourhood to get things done – help the unemployed, get a community centre, petition over bus services or road safety. Many of the myths of the council and its power-base have been dispelled. It isn't so intimidating . . . The limits of the council's power are visible; the cuts and limits imposed by central government become plainer.

Seen in this light, the neighbourhood offices provide what was described by one of their staff as 'a system of political education' so that people learn to have 'a little less faith in the experts and a bit more in themselves' (quoted in Seabrook, 1984, p. 142).

Seabrook's enthusiasm for such schemes of decentralization is not however universal on the left. There are those for whom decentralization falls into the trap of merely reproducing miniaturized versions of traditional organizations without seriously challenging the established social relations between different workers and between workers and users. Such criticisms for example are made by Beresford and Croft who address them specifically to the proposals for decentralization which have come from a number of left-wing local authorities. These proposals, they fear,

> seem to have been conceived predominantly in terms of changing buildings and structures – and then from one kind of local authority type structure to another, rather than with the guiding principle of enabling the transformation of relationships. (Beresford and Croft, 1984, p. 34)

A similar concern has been expressed by Wainwright (1984) to whom it appeared that decentralization was 'concerned primarily with improving the accessibility and responsiveness of state services'. The important task however was 'to change power relations . . . sharing power with community and workplace organisations and. helping to build their power'.

Popular planning

The advocates of going local do not of course accept that it is little more than an administrative reform. Maurice Barnes, the chair of the decentralization sub-committee at Islington, has been quite clear in his own mind that decentralization 'is a policy of confrontation [and] . . . a radical socialist challenge to those who write off the poor, the weak and the under privileged' (*Islington Neighbourhood News*, August 1984). Yet there are others on the left who, while accepting that 'decentralisation is needed', fear that 'the prospects for it living up to expectations . . . are poor' partly because it will inevitably be circumscribed by the limits of local authority powers and resources and partly because 'decentralisation is not a policy that comes from the people' but from enthusiastic councillors and activists (Beresford and Croft, 1983, pp. 26–7). From this perspective going local needs to be supplemented by other exercises in direct democracy, more especially since some of the decentralization proposals, while quite clear on reorganization of council service provision, are rather unclear on the mechanisms of local democratic control over the newly decentralized services in general and over their finances in particular.

One particular experiment in direct democracy, which has been taken up by the GLC, is that known as popular planning.

Popular planning is planning from below – planning that is based on people coming together in their workplace and community organisations to formulate their own demands and wishes for the future . . . Campaigns against redundancies and cuts, campaigns against hospital or nursery closures, campaigns for better heating on council estates – these are the first stages of popular planning. The second stage is the formulation of alternatives and the fight to put them into practice. (GLC, *Jobs for a Change* bulletin, June 1984)

The origins of popular planning lay outside the world of local government and had links with the experiences of workers producing 'alternative plans' at Lucas Aerospace and Vickers in the 1970s. A declaration *Popular Planning for Social Need* was published in 1981 jointly by Coventry Trades Council and the Lucas Aerospace Combine Shop Stewards Committee, on behalf of a number of other trades councils and combine committees. The declaration proposed

linking the social needs still unmet as a result of the rundown of public services, with the resources (particularly human resources) of the manufacturing, energy, and construction industries . . . The process of matching need with resources will have to be done 'from below' through workers and community based organisations drawing up their own plans, meeting their needs both as consumers and producers.

In political terms, as perceived by the GLC's Economic Policy Group, one part of the exercise 'is to bargain for plans, to fight for plans, and bits of those plans will be implemented. It is a strategy for opposition and it is a strategy for resistance' (Wainwright, 1983, p. 11). But it is more than being 'just anti', for 'We cannot challenge the decisions by governments or companies . . . *unless we develop our own vision, and strategy, for London's areas, industries and services*' (GLC, 1983b, pp. 65–6, emphasis in original).

The *People's Plan for the Royal Docks* is perhaps the first and clearest example of this approach, having arisen out of opposition from North Woolwich residents to the proposal for a STOL-port. The outcome was the publication of a plan for the Royal Docks area based on the proposition that Docklands should be planned in the interests of its own inhabitants and of identified social needs, rather than as a convenient annex to the nearby City of London and its financial institutions. Other initiatives, less confined to a single location, have been concerned with the creation of jobs and the meeting of needs in such fields as child care and home insulation and warmth.

The commitment of popular planning to the identification and matching of needs and resources 'from below' is seen to have two potential virtues. One of these is that

> each small project that gets off the ground, which brings together unemployed resources in socially useful production, shows that there is a socialist economics of commonsense . . . [that] gives the lie to Thatcherism and its doctrine that unemployment is inevitable. (Blazyca, 1983, pp. 97–8)

The other virtue is seen to lie in the potential 'to persuade people of their ability to make key decisions and to plan [which] is, or should be, a main plank of socialist and Labour Party argument' (Blazyca, 1983, p. 6). Thus whatever the material benefits might be that could accrue from popular planning, by way of jobs created, resources used and needs met, there would be a major growth in 'the confidence that working people have in their own ability to run things' (Blazyca, 1983, p. 105). In that sense popular planning is seen to have a major role to play as 'an educator and a, sort of, mobiliser' (Wainwright, 1983, p. 11).

Mobilization

A concern with political education and mobilization recurs through-out discussions of local socialism and it does so particularly in the context of certain social changes which are seen to have challenged some of the traditional working assumptions of Labour politics. The exact significance of these changes is itself sometimes a matter of dispute but their existence is widely recognized and the need for appropriate responses to them is accepted.

Thus for Jeremy Seabrook (1984, pp. 112, 147 and 4) one of the major virtues of the Walsall neighbourhood experiment lies in the possibility that it may lead to 'the regeneration of neighbourhood and community', to 'a first and tentative step in the cementing of a solidarity that is the only weapon of those who have nothing but their labour', thus reversing recent trends towards 'dissolving the old industrial communities' and with them their 'traditional working class values'. His perspective has drawn the criticism that it is 'moralising ... backward-looking and paternalistic ... the disgruntled argument of the born-again Muggeridges of the 1960s' (Croft and Beresford, 1984, p. 58). Certainly some of Seabrook's work has expressed profound regret that 'the majority of the working class seem to have accepted a growing dependency upon the values of capitalism', that 'the old working class has become an anachronism, a vestigial reminder', and that because 'our improvements have been achieved on the terms of capitalism ... there is nothing but discord and violence, ruined human relationships, the contamination, not only of work, but of neighbourhood, kinship and comradeliness, division between generations, distrust within families' (Seabrook, 1978, pp. 129, 244, 13–14). There is indeed in such a critique a sense that the workers have somehow let Seabrook down by not holding fast to his own rigorous standards. None the less he does draw attention to one major problem confronting the left, namely the decline of solidaristic working-class communities in many urban areas.

In his account of life in Hackney in the early 1980s Paul Harrison (1983, pp. 33, 236–7, 434) paints a stark picture of the inner city as a place of

> fragmentation – of communities, families and even individuals ... that can only be believed if witnessed ... a mass of conflicts and cleavages: young against old; delinquents against the law-abiding ... the quiet against the noisy ... rent-payers against squatters; taxpayers against claimants; black against white ... a score or more possible divisions, and most of them cut criss-cross through each other ... a chaos of individual and sectional pathologies and disruptions.

In less apocalyptic terms Dunleavy (1979, 1980) has identified the emergence of one important new line of political cleavage which cuts across that based on occupational class divisions. He refers to the public/private sector cleavage between those who work in and/or gain access to goods and services through the two different sectors and argues that a voter's self-identification with one or other sector has played a major part in blurring previous links between class and party. He also suggests that such sectoral fragmentation may be most pronounced within the working class since it is there that there have emerged recently some of the major cleavages in consumption sector location with the spread of car and home ownership. In the specific context of local politics, Saunders (1981, pp. 275–6) has argued that

> urban struggles are constituted in the sphere of consumption on the basis of specific sectoral interests which may or may not coincide with class alignments . . . they are mainly locally based, and . . . tend to be both issue-specific and locality-specific. In short urban struggles are typically fragmented . . . localized . . . strategically limited . . . and politically isolated.

It is certainly not difficult to see evidence of social fragmentation and diversity in a variety of forms. The growth of the domestic, informal and black economies, of self-help and voluntary action, of diverse religions and cults, of ethnic and generational sub-cultures, and of often ephemeral popular fashions may all be seen as pointers in this direction. So, too, may the emergence of the various 'separatist' demands for women-only facilities, for black sections in the Labour Party, for bans on trans-racial adoption and for own-language teaching in schools. Each of these phenomena may have their own separate rationale but taken collectively, along with sectoral cleavages, they suggest a society increasingly characterized by social pluralism rather than class solidarity. Such developments can clearly have quite marked political consequences and Labour's general election defeats of 1979 and 1983 stimulated considerable debate on what these might be.

The debate had really begun in September 1978, with the appearance in *Marxism Today* of Eric Hobsbawm's Marx Memorial Lecture, *The Forward March of Labour Halted?* He feared there was 'a growing division of workers into sections and groups, each pursuing its own interest irrespective of the rest' and also that 'the manual working class core of traditional socialist labour parties is today contracting and not expanding' (Hobsbawm, 1981, p. 14 and 1982, p. 11). The exact implications of his analysis became a subject of considerable argument, especially when, after Labour's 1983 election defeat, he was taken to be suggesting the need for a broad anti-Thatcher alliance rather than one specifically committed to socialist goals (Hobsbawm, 1983). Others placed more stress on building alliances not towards the centre but towards the left, embracing 'the many socialist groups that have appeared on the scene, often with their own newspapers and campaigns' (Benn, 1983, p. 35). There had however been a growing feeling amongst many on the left that one particular task for Labour was 'to articulate the needs of the minorities and the dispossessed . . . as well as the interests of the organised working class' and to recognize the importance of single-issue groups since 'increasingly people are themselves aligned to one of these smaller groupings rather than in the sort of broad class concepts that people saw themselves [in] thirty years ago' (Livingstone, 1981, p. 18).

Such an approach clearly echoed one of the points made by the advocates of extra-parliamentary politics and cited in an earlier chapter, namely *London Labour Briefing*'s demand in June 1982 that Labour councillors should 'link up with . . . the trade unions, ethnic minority organisations, women's movement, tenants' and residents' organisations, etc., etc.'. Hain and Hebditch (1978, p. 8), too, had previously identified groups whose involvement in radical politics had largely by-passed the Labour Party – 'community groups, claimants' unions, women's liberation, black groups . . . environmentalists, radical professionals, and the "counter-culture" ' – and had urged that Labour should find ways of responding to their needs. With many of these groups being organized on a very localized basis, and often seeking help from, or having problems with, their local authority, the role of Labour councils could be seen as potentially a crucial one. Such councils could begin the process of trying to build new social alliances or a new coalition which could simultaneously attempt to re-unite divided communities while also creating a broader political constituency for the Labour Party than that represented by its traditional supporters alone.

It is not however self-evident that the creation of such a new social alliance would in itself necessarily assist in the process of socialist transformation. A mass party based on a large working class with a common life-style and a tradition of collective action did seem, historically, a possible engine of long-term socialist advance. In contrast, a coalition of varied groups, based upon, and distinguished from one another by, differences of class, generation, life-style, race, culture, housing tenure, job market status, sexual proclivity, family circumstances, and issue orientation might seem more likely to re-create the catch-all, log-rolling politics of the Democratic and Republican parties of the USA. Whatever their virtues in a multi-cultural, multi-racial society it has rarely been suggested that parties of such a type were plausible engines of long-term social transformation as distinct from piecemeal social engineering. There was of course one attempt to employ an American party very much in the manner now being suggested on the left. Indeed Ken Livingstone

(1981, p. 17) recognized that what was being suggested in Britain was 'very similar in a sense to the sort of alliance that backed George McGovern in 1972 against Richard Nixon'. McGovern placed his faith in a party whose internal structure had been reformed to give greater power to the rank and file activists, who in turn endorsed a strategy directed towards a 'new politics' of the young, the black and the poor. The end result, however, was political disaster and electoral humiliation: not an auspicious omen perhaps, especially since a major cause of the defeat lay in the defection of blue-collar and trade union voters, alienated by the style as much as by the substance of the new politics.

However, it may be argued that to take such a gloomy view of the prospects of any new coalition is to be guilty of what E. P. Thompson (1974, pp. 99–100) has described as 'the fixity of concept which characterises much capitalist ideology', seeing people and their organizations as they appear under capitalism as the sole possible reality, and ignoring any latent potential for change which might be made manifest by a raising of the level of consciousness. This argument brings us to the second major strategy of local socialism, namely the transforming of popular consciousness through a process of mobilization, thereby 'shifting the general climate of opinion to the left' (Clarke and Griffiths, 1982, p. 9).

The precise nature of the mobilization being envisaged is not always clear. Both the insurrectionary and the parliamentary routes are discounted, not least because of their tendencies to elitism in the respective forms of revolutionary vanguards and ministerial oligarchies trying to impose socialism from above. Instead the emphasis is on 'a more activist role in the community, going outwards and involving people rather than preaching down at them' (Beresford and Croft, 1982, p. 2). In Walsall for example it was hoped that popular involvement with the neighbourhood offices 'would make people more persuadable to our political viewpoint' (Nicholas, 1981, p. 6). Similarly the hope was expressed in *London Labour Briefing* (August 1982) that decentralization would 'help develop a political awareness' that local struggles 'are a common anti-capitalist struggle'. There are however problems when a strategy of mobilization is linked with one of decentralization: they may be summarized as the problems of populism, pluralism and pre-ceptoralism.

Hain (1980b, p. 9) has warned that 'it would, of course, be easy to degenerate into mere populism as has been the case for the vast majority of the Liberals' "community politics" newsheets': Beresford and Croft (1982, p. 2), have feared 'another misplaced bout of left populism'. Now populism is a notoriously slippery concept, and it is not wholly clear how it is being used here. In one sense, of course, the whole idea of the politically committed 'going outwards and involving people' is highly redolent of that specific form of populism which occurred in late nineteenth-century Russia when middle-class members of Land and Liberty were urged: 'Steep yourself in the great sea of the people. Throw open your eyes and your ears' (quoted in Canovan, 1981, p. 79). However, the references to a 'misplaced' or 'mere' populism suggest, not fears of a replay of the harsh fate of Russian populism, but rather an anxiety to avoid an unprincipled pandering to what are seen as the more selfish, reactionary and chauvinistic views which can be found in the pubs, clubs and bingo halls. This is of course the problem posed by such a figure as Enoch Powell and by George Wallace, of whom it was said:

> He is talking about poor people, 'ordinary folks' ... you might mistake him for a New Left advocate of the poverty program, urging the maximum feasible participation of the poor and the return of local government to the people. (Lipset and Raab, 1979, p. 342)

If decentralization of power to the people were to result in their mobilizing themselves in favour of localized displays of racism, economic beggar-my-neighbour, and 'scrounger' bashing it would hardly represent a major step forward in socialist transformation. Yet even without taking such a bleak view of the likelihood of a reactionary populism it is still possible to imagine that popular mobilization could fall short of the socialist goal.

There is a possibility that, given the necessary power, people may do with it what they will; and while that may not necessarily take the form of a Gadarene descent into rabid reaction, it may not be socialism either. Indeed, given the kaleidoscopic variety of groups within the community to whom that power might be decentralized, it is not implausible to suggest that it may result in a variety of preferred patterns of policies and resource allocation amongst the various groups.

Here we encounter the problem of pluralism with the possibility that the 'people' and the various groups which are its several manifestations, may, once mobilized and armed with power, choose to go their own several ways: and those ways may not necessarily lead to a socialist transformation, though some may be in varying ways quite benign, or at least harmless. Thus, to the fear of a possibly reactionary populism, there may be added the uncertainties of pluralism, with local communities and groups seizing the gift of power offered by the new urban left yet employing the gift for varying purposes, not always those intended by the donor. Such might be the outcome, for example, if Saunders (1982, p. 65) is correct in his judgement about 'local consumption struggles ... fragmenting political mobilization into a series of competitive sectoral conflicts'.

How can this be avoided, if socialist transformation is to take place? To withhold real power from the grass roots unless certain of its use for socialist purposes would be one possibility: yet, in the words of one GLC committee chairman, to do so would be a left-wing equivalent of 'setting up Bantustans', granting the trappings rather than the reality of power. Some other solution is required, which will enable the processes of decentralization and mobilization to acquire a sense of socialist direction, for 'a socialist decentralisation will require the explicit injection of socialist values into every stage and all aspects' (Labour Co-ordinating Committee, 1984, p. 36).

The answer is to be found in the role of the local party activists. It will not be enough merely to encourage wider participation or maximum decentralization amongst the people at large. What is needed instead is a process of 'involving ordinary people and party activists in struggles for power' (Hain, 1980b, p. 9), of 'giving "power to the people", with extensive party involvement' as one activist expressed it in *London Labour Briefing* in August 1982. Decentralization 'would be a spur to Labour party members and other socialists to be more active locally and convince people that their policies were in people's interests' (Labour Co-ordinating Committee, 1984, p. 32). The presence of the party and its activists is, presumably, required in order to awaken the people to the possibilities of local socialism whenever they are in danger of straying in other directions.

This approach has its antecedents in the experiences of community action, where deprived communities were seen as needing a stimulus for action 'from the middle class community activist who brings to the situation an ideology and certain skills in understanding the existing state of affairs and in explaining ways in which he thinks this state of affairs might be changed' (Baine, 1975, p. 87). It had parallels too amongst the *groupes d'action municipale* in France in the 1970s. In Louviers the victorious *comité d'action de gauche* proclaimed its determination to 'educate' the people about the political dangers emanating from other quarters (Brown, 1982, p. 118), while in Mons-en-Baroeul local socialists saw the 'raising of consciousness' as a necessary feature of local self-determination (Loew, 1980, p. 2). Such tactics might indeed overcome the problems of the emergence of a reactionary populism or a non-socialist pluralism but they do raise difficulties of their own. For their essentially tutelary nature seems to imply the adoption of what Lindblom (1977, p. 59) has described as a 'preceptoral' form of politics, elements of which he finds particularly, though not exclusively, in Mao's China and Castro's Cuba:

In a preceptoral system rationality rests on an ideology which once taught to the individual gives him both a 'correct' understanding of the social world and guidelines for his own decisions. Although a preceptoral system depends on simple moral and emotional appeals to supplement the rational, the core element in the creation of the new man is his ideological education, a genuine attempt to raise the level of his conscious, thoughtful, deliberated understanding. For members of the party, a high level of consciousness is all the more demanded. They must speak, write, and publish. All this is possible because 'education' is usually intended to help men discover many of their true or objective interests, not typically to hoodwink or exploit them.

Preceptoral politics would seem to have much in common with the style of politics embraced by the new urban left. For one thing, 'all preceptoral systems are mobilization systems'; for another it rejects the notion of social co-ordination through bureaucracy or through the invisible hand of the market, implying instead a 'substantial decentralization of decision making, . . . [and] a great deal of mutual adjustment . . . among ordinary citizens and cadres [activists]' (Lindblom, 1977, pp. 58 and 60).

The assumption is that all other existing systems are grossly wasteful, because they fail to tap individual energies and resource-fulness . . . the preceptoral vision . . . aims at a revolutionary reorganisation of human energies by making much of what other systems underplay. (Lindblom, 1977, pp. 60–1)

The key to the operation of a preceptoral system is the process of persuasion. Such a system may be presented as one in which both preceptors and people, the teachers and the taught, embark on a journey of mutual discovery. Yet as Lindblom (1977, p. 62) observes 'one can be cynical about the preceptoral aspiration itself, for all over the world men who want authority look for improved ways to disguise it'. Bureaucratic and market-based authority may by now be too naked and too widely disparaged. But what of the intellectually-based authority of the benevolent and persuasive preceptor?

At the heart of a preceptoral system of politics there lies both an absurdity and a danger. The absurdity lies in rejecting the claim of the traditional professionals to possess a correct scientific understanding of some single aspect of society – urban planning, housing, health – while simultaneously claiming for oneself the possession of a correct scientific understanding of the entire structure and processes of the whole society. The danger of preceptoral politics lies in the fact that whatever its hopes for mutual adjustment and mutual discovery it rests on one implicit assumption related to the project of consciousness-raising.

'Consciousness raising' is a project of higher-class individuals directed at a lower-class population. It is the latter, *not* the former whose consciousness is to be raised. What is more, the consciousness at issue is the consciousness that the lower-class population has of *its own situation*. Thus a crucial assumption of the concept is that lower-class people do not understand their own situation, that they are in need of enlightenment on the matter, and that this service can be provided by selected higher-class individuals. (Berger, 1977, pp. 137–8, emphasis in original)

Thus when an article in *London Labour Briefing* in August 1982 spoke of 'our hopes' that decentralization would 'help develop a political awareness among more people' that their various local struggles were 'a common anti-capitalist struggle', the underlying assumption was that 'we' had seen a light which 'they' had yet to recognize. Moreover, those to whom the light had been revealed can easily find themselves regarding that light not merely as an arguably more or less correct hypothesis but as a true correspondence of reality, as 'scientific' rather than 'ideological', seeing it as somehow privileged, in a secular version of the way in which Catholic theology accorded 'truth' greater rights and status than 'error'. Such, for example, were the views of the preceptors of Mao's Cultural Revolution, expressed in the *May 16 Circular* of 1967:

In the struggle between proletariat and bourgeoisie, between Marxist truth and the lies of the bourgeois class and of all oppressive classes, if the east wind does not prevail over the west wind, the west wind will prevail over the east wind, and therefore no equality can exist between them. (Quoted in Leys, 1978, p. 131)

An attitude like that can make it all too easy for the preceptor to see his activity not as one of imposing his own views on others, or as a process of converting people from one to another of a number of competing views, but simply as one of enabling others to recognize, acknowledge and act upon the single objective reality with which he himself is already familiar but which for others is disguised by various mystifications.

Thus against the 'fixity of concept' of capitalist ideology there is placed

the assumption that science – that is, the 'social science' of Marxism – can liberate men from the encumbrances of all past institutions, family ties, social loyalties, professional affiliations, and religious and philosophical commitments: first by exposing these as 'unscientific', then by demonstrating that they are no longer necessary in a truly 'scientific' environment. (Lifton, 1967, p. 521)

To take such a view, however, is to 'look upon human beings, at least implicitly, as wrongly-moulded clay, needing only new moulds and proper remoulding from ideological potters' (Lifton, 1967, p. 525). There is a danger in such a view of humanity, a danger no less serious than that attendant upon the belief that capitalist man is the only man. The danger is simply that preceptoralism, no matter how benign its intent, may, under pressure, degenerate into a manipulative elitism. The task of 'persuasion', if it is seeking to bring about a major shift in human consciousness, is a difficult one, and as Lindblom (1977, p. 56) observes, the very word persuasion

> hardly does justice to the variety of persuasive communications employed in the preceptoral system. Persuasion, information, indoctrination, instruction, propaganda, counselling, advice, exhortation, education and thought control constitute the range of methods used to induce the desired responses.

Preceptors who see themselves as possessors of an objectively true socialist consciousness, superior to the false consciousness of the less enlightened, may be prey to the temptation of employing the more domineering forms of persuasion, the more so if the people at large seem liable to veer in the direction of populism, pluralism or some other 'erroneous' course. Those to whom the truth has been revealed can sometimes be rather impatient with those who seem slow, or even unable, to see the light, and can all too easily assume that they, the enlightened, alone know what is best. Moreover, if the views of party activists are taken to be 'really' representative of the objective interests of the people, regardless of the actual views of the latter, then it is all too easy for them to begin that process which equates party and people, thereby reducing the very real problem of accountability to the people to the no less real, but very different, problem of accountability to the party.

The elevation of the party activist, in his preceptoral role, to a key position in local politics is a logical concomitant of the extra-parliamentary strategy of socialist transformation through mass mobilization. The new urban left, as part of a broader extra-parliamentary movement, represents an attempt to use local government as a base from which to chart a road to socialism which will avoid both the insurrectionary elitism of revolutionary vanguards and the parliamentary elitism of ministerial oligarchies. It would be ironical however if, in trying to do so, it succumbed to the temptations of a preceptoral elitism of party activists.

Such problems of the relationship between the people and the party and its activists are of course acknowledged by some on the left. Members of the Labour Co-ordinating Committee in particular have argued that 'socialists should be committed to the *principle* of people controlling their own lives, whether or not we like all the immediate results' and that 'if opening up local government isn't going to be a phoney exercise then it does mean accepting that some of the decisions local committees will take won't always be the ones we would have preferred' (Clarke and Griffiths, 1982, p. 24, emphasis in original; Labour Co-ordinating Committee, 1984, p. 32). There have been warnings too of the tendency which 'sees the only important democracy as the democracy of the Labour Party' and which maintains 'that only the Labour Party can be trusted to run these things and that people who are not Party members should not have certain important political rights' (Clarke and Griffiths, 1982, p. 5).

However not all those on the left would agree with such an open-handed approach. Liverpool in particular has seen the party elevated to a central position in the decision-making process. As far as the council is concerned the chairman of the District Labour Party has proclaimed that:

the District Labour Party is the policy-making body but also the Labour group implement that policy and the Liverpool District Party elect the Leader, Deputy Leader and the Chairman of key positions in the Labour Group, a position which as far as I know is unparalleled. (Mulhearn, 1984)

As for the city outside the council:

If there is a contribution through the party we will meet with anybody to explain and defend our policies – but we are not consensus people. We believe that the party – democratically elected – makes the policy and the Labour group carries it out. (Councillor Tony Byrne, *Guardian*, 7 August 1984)

In such circumstances there was little or no role for such bodies as local community groups or housing co-operatives and some members of the latter began to consider that joining the Labour Party was the only way to influence council policy (Grosskurth, 1985). One dissenting Liverpool Labour activist, whilst supporting the 'continual mobilisation of labour voters behind a militant defence of jobs and services', described the local party's attitude as one of 'party chauvinism' which assumed that 'socialism *is* the Labour Party running the local authority, and [that] if local people want to influence policy they should join the party' (Thompson, 1984, emphasis in original).

The nature of what is being attempted in Liverpool, which is clearly consistent with the notion of giving a leading role to the party, has aroused some controversy on the left. Thus one Labour councillor, referring to the key role of the council's Performance Review and Financial Control Sub-Committee, claimed that 'the apparent development of a "Central Committee" is worrying a number of comrades both inside and outside the group' (*Merseyside Labour Briefing*, July 1983). A similar, though differently expressed, fear was uttered in 1984 by another activist who spoke of 'a common feeling . . . that the Labour Group's leadership is beginning to act like the old "city bosses", who thought the job of voters was to vote, and theirs was to make decisions' (*New Statesman*, 26 October 1984). Nevertheless, such criticisms cannot gainsay the fact that Liverpool Labour councillors have made strenuous attempts to mobilize popular support by going out into the community. In 1983 for example the controlling Labour group organized numerous public meetings about schools reorganization. In 1984 two series of meetings were arranged at ward level – eighteen in two weeks in February 1984 and again in June and July 1984 for example – together with workplace and factory gate meetings to mobilize support for the council over its budget crisis. There was also much Labour activity in the form of leafleting and canvassing, to the point where some local Liberals began to feel they were being outflanked at the business of doorstep politics.

Thus major efforts at public consultation and participation do take place in Liverpool: however such exercises do have their own characteristic form.

> We have full canvasses, and many wards put out five or six leaflets explaining national, city-wide and local issues ... [P]ublic meetings ... are vital because as well as attracting new support they help to draw together the active workers and raise morale all round. (Hatton, 1984)

> Hundreds of people are turning up to their local meeting to listen to the council's case, ask questions, and talk individually to their councillors afterwards. (Dunlop, 1984)

Such exercises clearly allow the public to learn what the local authority has in mind; they permit the doubters to ask questions; and they allow individuals to talk, in Dunlop's phrase 'on a one to one basis with their local councillors'. But they do not seem designed to encourage debate, or to allow the canvassing of alternative strategies or to facilitate the mobilization of dissent from what is proposed. The emphasis on 'explaining', on 'attracting new support', on 'drawing together', on 'raising morale' and on 'listening to the council's case' suggests that the major concern is to mobilize the people behind the line already identified as correct by the council, or more accurately by the local Labour Party. There are strange echoes here of some of the more circumscribed forms of public participation in planning in the 1960s and 1970s in which professional planners sought to build up a constituency of support for particular planning proposals rather than to encourage genuinely open debate about the underlying problems. Indeed such exercises have in the past been condemned on the left as forms of pseudo-participation mainly aimed at mobilizing people into support for the policies of those already in power. Hain (1980a, p. 23) for example argued that such forms of participation 'can be understood in terms of a process of "mobilisation" of support upwards from the populace rather than a redistribution of power or influence downwards to the citizen'. Hain's criticism was echoed by an academic study which concluded that in a variety of local services 'participation has served the purposes of building up a consensus for the proposals of those in power' (Boaden et al., 1982, p. 179). It is not immediately obvious that the charge is any the less appropriate when those who are in positions of power come from the left of politics. Mobilizing support upwards rather than redistributing power downwards does not become any the more democratic when it is done by the political left than when it is done by the political right or by the professional local government establishment.

It might be the case that such a situation is the singular product of the party chauvinism of the Liverpool left. Events in Sheffield in 1980 and 1981 however raise similar questions about the nature of popular participation under local socialism. When school governors, teachers, parents and children were consulted following the 1980 local elections about Labour's commitment to abolish both school uniforms and corporal punishment, they were under the impression that they were actually being asked for their opinions on the merits of the policies. To the Labour Party however 'they were assumed to be accepted policy, having been voted upon by the electorate' (David Blunkett, Sheffield Star, 6 October 1981). Accordingly people were merely being asked 'how best to put into practice what has been decided' (Blunkett, 1984, p. 250). The upshot was confusion and ill-feeling between the public and the politicians and a classic instance of politically, rather than professionally, circumscribed participation.

The case of Liverpool in particular highlights the fact that there can well be a tension between the two processes of mobilization and participation; and in so far as decentralization is seen as a means to maximize participation, there can thus be a tension between the two strategies of mobilization and decentralization. It may therefore be no accident that Liverpool has not been very keen on decentralization, for the latter might somehow impede or confuse the process of mobilization. The hidden political dangers which could underlie a programme of decentralization were aptly summed up by an Islington councillor during a fringe meeting on the subject at the 1983

Greater London Labour Party conference: 'The big neurosis which grips everyone is fear of losing control'. The idea of decentralizing power without at the same time losing at least a measure of control might be thought to be a contradiction in terms. The posing of the problem in such a fashion is illuminating however since it exposes what Robert Heilbroner has described as a 'fundamental uncertainty' within socialism.

To Heilbroner 'what is attractive to the radical mind in the conception of socialism is above all the idea that a socialist society is best suited for the active development of the human capacity for self-determination'. Such a notion of socialism as 'a vehicle for human self-direction' might be thought to imply 'the freest expression of individuality in art, in sexual and social relations, in political thought and act'. Yet this seems to conflict with the vision of socialism which 'applies the collective wisdom and judgement of the community in establishing *norms* of behaviour, *shared* moral standards, a *unifying* vision of the good life'. Heilbroner's conclusion is that if socialism really is serious about self-determination and self-direction then 'a socialist society must reconcile itself to an indeterminate space within which men can express their wishes and drives, *whether or not these conform to the ideals and goals of socialism itself*' (Heilbroner, 1972, pp. 465 and 469, emphasis in original). It is in the implicit pluralism of his conclusions that Heilbroner anticipates what might seem a basic dilemma of local socialism, namely whether its chief political strategy is to be one of decentralizing in order to disperse power in a variety of directions or of mobilizing in order to concentrate it in a single direction.

5   Prospects

Capitalist societies in general do require a measure of apathy . . .
But socialist societies, like ancient republics, require relatively
high levels of civic virtue in their citizens. (John Dunn, 1984, p. 69)

The emergence of local socialism in the early 1980s can be
interpreted in various ways. It can be seen as one product of certain
major social and generational changes in the composition of the
Labour Party with new activists introducing new preoccupations and
new values. Such changes are not wholly peculiar to that party, since
other Western socialist and labour parties have experienced similar
changes. It can also be understood as one element in a wider reaction
against, or at least dissatisfaction with, some elements of the
post-1945 welfare state consensus, which has expressed itself in an
enthusiasm for decentralist ideas at various points on the political
spectrum, not only in Britain but in other countries as well.

Additionally, local socialism can be seen as a reaction to four crises
occurring in conjunction during the 1970s and into the 1980s. They
are the fiscal crisis of local government; the social crisis of the inner
cities; the electoral crisis of the Labour Party; and the ideological
crisis of socialism. From the left's perspective the conjunction of
these crises converted local government from a necessary but rather
mundane activity into a political challenge, a challenge in that it was
the source simultaneously of problems to be tackled and of possible
opportunities to be seized. The fiscal and social crises created
problems of defending established services and those who depended
upon them. The electoral and ideological crises encouraged a search
for new political constituencies and new conceptions of socialism,
both of which might be secured through a more localist orientation.

Seen from the perspective of local government, local socialism
could be viewed as forming one part of a much wider reappraisal of
traditional assumptions about the roles and workings of local
authorities. We have already seen how, on both the left and right of
politics, there has developed a mood of scepticism and sometimes
hostility towards local government bureaucracy and professionalism.
This has formed part of a broader development of an ideological local
politics, threatening to displace the administrative politics of an
earlier era. The spread of an increasingly ideological local politics has
in turn reflected the ideological polarization undergone by the two
major political parties during a period when party-dominated local

government has become almost universal other than in the remoter rural areas.

Both the Labour left and the Conservative right have brought new ideas into local government, ideas whose implementation entails considerable changes in conventional local authority practice. The left's concern with developing new roles for local government in such fields as the local economy, race policies and women's issues have been accompanied by the enthusiasm of the new right for a reduction in the role of local authorities through schemes of privatization in such spheres as street cleaning, rent collection, recreation management, highway maintenance, adoption services and care of the elderly. Similarly the left's commitment to extending a greater influence in local government decision-making to the trades unions, to local Labour parties and to certain local community groups has been followed by the Thatcher government's Rates Act 1984, which requires local authorities to consult representatives of industrial and commercial ratepayers each year about proposals for council expenditures and their finance.

The common theme of such developments lies in their representing a move away from a form of what C. P. Snow used to call 'closed politics' towards a more 'open politics' in which the councils' links with, and even dependence upon, elements of the wider economic and social structure become major features of its decision-making. Clearly such open-ness is far from total, and its character depends upon the particular political bias of individual local authorities. None the less, in moving from closed politics towards open politics local government may also experience changes additional to those entailed in the move from administrative to ideological politics.

If service delivery through privatization or decentralization to wards or neighbourhoods were to gather pace, and if local authorities were increasingly to become sources of contracts, franchises and grant-funding then the tasks of dealing with agents and clients and of resource allocation and co-ordination might begin to look very like the bargaining politics which Hill (1972, pp. 217–26) noted as particularly characteristic of local government in the United States. They might indeed also take on overtones of that other common feature of American local government, namely, patronage politics.

The displacement, or at least the supplementation, of administrative politics by ideological politics, open politics, bargaining politics and patronage politics would change both the ethos and the day-to-day workings of local government in Britain. Such changes would clearly be matters of consequence for those who are involved directly in local government themselves. Yet for the proponents of local socialism it is likely that such changes are of only secondary importance. Their main concern is with the political prospects for the local road to socialism. To speculate on those prospects is certainly to create hostages to fortune: yet the attempt to do so may at least help to crystallize some of the key issues that are posed by local socialism.

A 'brief idea'?

Some years ago *New Society* (22 September 1977) published a symposium on 'A History of Brief Ideas' in which it explored a number of ideas and initiatives in education, social services, housing, architecture, planning, economics, the health service and local government, all of which had seemed a good idea at the time but which had eventually failed to live up to expectations or had even proved to be downright failures. Industrialized building, Nuffield science teaching and the reorganizations of the health service and of local government were among the political and professional enthusiasms singled out as ventures which at best left hopes unfulfilled and at worst proved to have been largely counter-productive. The reference in the previous chapter to guild socialism and syndicalism in 1914 provided another example of a rather different form of brief idea, namely one whose hour came, and then suddenly went, without its potential ever being properly explored.

Clearly political enthusiasms do come and go, either aborted at an early stage or rejected in the light of their eventual failure. Monetarism, it might reasonably be thought, is a prime candidate for the latter category of failed brief ideas. But what of local socialism – are there possible pitfalls which might consign it, too, to the lost world of brief ideas?

Political defeat

One possibility which must be contemplated is that of a major defeat of some sort at the hands of the present Conservative government, specifically over the issue of rate-capping, which has been generally seen by its opponents as a more important long-term threat than abolition of the GLC and the metropolitan counties. For even if those authorities were to be saved they too could then fall victim to rate-capping in their turn. The wide measure of agreement reached at the re-called Labour local government conference at Sheffield in July 1984 seemed to pave the way for the development of a united strategy for opposing the government. The refusal to enter into individual negotiations with the Secretary of State, Patrick Jenkin, over 1985/6 expenditure levels and rate levels under the terms of the Rates Act

1984, was adhered to by all the 16 Labour councils on the list of authorities due to have their rates capped, although at one point Lewisham seemed to be flirting with the idea of talks. However, once the deadline for such negotiations had passed the problem of maintaining unity then became focused on the more complicated issues of rate-setting and budget-making for 1985/6. Moreover the policy of non-compliance, while merely involving non-co-operation with the government in the case of negotiations could well imply defiance of the law in the case of rate-setting and budget-making, a step about which Labour's parliamentary leadership was a good deal less enthusiastic than was the 1984 party conference.

Two main strategies were offered. One was the 'no-rate' strategy, whereby an authority would refuse to fix a rate but would continue to provide services for as long as it could, if necessary defaulting on interest payments to financial institutions in order to fund service provision. This so-called 'London option', originally favoured at Sheffield by the leaders of the GLC and seven London boroughs, was seen to have the advantage of enabling councils all to take a no-rate decision on a single given day and thereby confront the government with a clear crisis and a united front. The other strategy entailed producing a 'no-cuts' budget but levying the rate in accordance with the rate-capping requirement: a variant of this, favoured in Hackney, involved a no-cuts budget and a rate level in line with inflation (which would itself exceed the rate-capped level). Such deficit budgeting strategies would immediately reveal substantial gaps between income and expenditure and again precipitate financial crises, though at different times in different places as the money ran out and reserves were used up. A third possibility, identified by ILEA, was simply to ignore rate-capping and to match a no-cuts budget with a rate level above the legal limit. Underpinning all such strategies a campaign to mobilize popular support for Labour councils and the services they provide was also envisaged in the hope of strengthening the hand of the front-line authorities in their confrontation with the government.

Labour's 1985 local government conference at Birmingham in February revealed that the no-rate strategy had become the favourite option. The legal complexities, and perhaps even more so the legal uncertainties, seemed formidable: in discussions during Labour's Nottingham local government conference, for example, it appeared that lawyers could not agree on whether a local authority could actually go bankrupt, nor on what, if it could, would happen thereafter. For top-tier councils such as the GLC, the ILEA and the metropolitan counties the no-rate option faced the problem, not shared by lower-tier councils, of their having a legal obligation to fix a rate precept by a fixed date in March. In all cases the various strategies raised possibilities of the sending in of government commissioners to run local authorities and of surcharges on councillors and their disqualification from office.

Part of the problem lay in the need not merely to build solidarity amongst councils, but also amongst councillors. The sixteen rate-capped councils embraced several hundred Labour councillors, not all of whom, for personal, family or political reasons, could readily contemplate surcharge or disqualification. One solution to this difficulty which was canvassed, and occasionally implemented, was asking for or encouraging the resignation of councillors unwilling to risk illegality and replacing them at by-elections by those less inhibited.

In committing themselves to the course of non-compliance and possible illegality many on the left drew inspiration from the earlier efforts of Liverpool and the GLC; yet it is far from clear that those two instances provided appropriate precedents on which to build a strategy of confrontation leading beyond the law. Although skilful publicity had given Liverpool the appearance of victory in their 1984 contest with Patrick Jenkin the reality was far less one-sided. Liverpool had ended up with a 17 per cent rate rise (against 9 per cent originally intended), had abandoned its £2 decorating allowance for tenants and had agreed a far from radical capitalization of housing repairs; on the other hand Jenkin had continued to provide a measure of rate support grant, had soothed the money markets about Liverpool's credit standing, had kept the auditors and any possible commissioners at bay and had eventually struck a deal much of which however fell within terms available to any inner city partnership authority. The fact that the roof did not fall in – or the auditors and commissioners arrive – immediately after Liverpool's initial decision not to set a rate for 1984/5 was of course a major psychological victory for the council and contributed to a general sense of having got Jenkin on the run. Yet the eventual deal was an old-fashioned compromise rather than a major breakthrough, while the whole experience provided the Department of the Environment, as well as Liverpool and others, with a possibly useful rehearsal for future contests.

As for the campaign to save the GLC it is true that this struck a very responsive chord with the public, who rallied to the council's defence in large numbers. Yet this campaign was waged very much on the public's terms rather than on the specifically socialist terms of a left-wing GLC. It was an essentially defensive campaign, geared to reflect the findings of opinion polling, and thus appealing primarily to certain conventional but deeply-held public views about local democracy and the need for an elected body to represent London as a whole. Such an exercise did not necessarily provide a model for the very different task of building and sustaining a campaign of support for confrontation and possible illegality by councils committed to non-compliance with rate-capping.

The previous history of left-wing councils confronting Conservative governments gave little reason to suppose that solidarity would be readily achieved or sustained. When Clay Cross defied the Housing Finance Act 1972 it was the last survivor of over forty councils which had originally promised not to put the legislation into operation. Reference has already been made in the opening chapter to the gradual crumbling of local authority resistance on the issue of public assistance payments in 1931 and 1932 as councils decided to 'do what we can' rather than hand over to 'an arbitrary Commissioner'.

Two factors perhaps distinguished the would-be non-compliers of 1984 and 1985 from their predecessors. One was that they were better prepared ideologically for the journey into extra-parliamentary action and confrontation. Yet although this might be psychologically important for those who were actually likely to be in the firing line, it was not always clear to those who might be potential supporters just what the end of the journey might be. The shape of possible victory was never wholly clear other than at the level of rhetoric. The other factor was a clear recognition of the need to involve the local government unions to the maximum extent in any campaign. Yet recognition was one thing: securing the allegiance of rank and file union members was quite another, especially if they were being asked to endorse financial policies whose impact on their own jobs and pay packets was unclear. In any case the relations between the unions and left-wing councils had proved to be far from easy and whatever the outcome of the battle over rate-capping this uneasy relationship was in itself another possible source of problems for local socialism.

Internal divisions

In terms of morale and of room for political manoeuvre the struggle over rate-capping, and its resolution, were always likely to be significant in their impact on local socialism. Yet a clear victory did not in itself guarantee the future, for other factors might lead to local socialism failing in some way to meet either the aspirations of its adherents or the needs of those whom it could serve.

One set of problems is that which has been revealed by the occasional instances of political division leading to paralysis or stalemate which have afflicted some councils. It is here that relations with the unions play a part. Despite some attempts to involve the unions more closely in decision-making it is noticeable that a number of left-wing councils have found themselves involved in industrial disputes. Sheffield, St Helen's, Camden, Hackney, Islington, Lewisham and Southwark were all affected in this way at various times during 1983 and 1984. Problems of introducing new technology or new patterns of work have often underlain these disputes and their handling has sometimes revealed the existence of serious mistrust between unions and councillors. In Sheffield for example the introduction of new working conditions in the housing department led not only to a strike of over 600 staff but also to the accusation that some members of the council's Labour group 'intend to smash the union organisation' (*The Times*, 10 October 1984): the leader of the council for his part rejected the idea of the unions 'having a veto on the party manifesto' (quoted in Wolmar, 1984, p. 15). We have already seen in Chapter 4, how progress on decentralization has been delayed by union resistance in Hackney and in Islington. In Hackney itself a bitter dispute over the repairs service produced a four-way confrontation between the council, the tenants, the white-collar unions and the manual-worker unions in the course of which a NUPE shop steward, who was also an Islington councillor, declared that his prime objective was to bring down the leadership of Hackney council (*Community Action*, August–September 1984).

Such internecine strife amongst the various wings of the Labour movement is clearly not conducive to the successful pursuit of radical policies which may well disturb established practices, many of the latter perhaps representing the jealously guarded fruits of earlier union campaigns. The strife can however also reflect not only defensive attitudes by the unions but also manoeuvrings for political advantage amongst the various far-left groupings inside and outside the Labour Party. Such manoeuvrings are not of course confined to the unions although the SWP in particular have seen the latter as useful arenas for their small number of activists: for them decentralization policies in particular are dismissed as irrelevant – 'do it yourself cuts' – and local socialism in general as yet another blind alley of reformism whose eventual failure will provide more recruits for 'true' socialism.

Pressure and agitation from the left is not confined of course to that which comes from beyond the limits of the Labour Party. There are also attempts at outflanking on the left which occur within the party. Margaret Hodge has identified

the strategy of raising demands that cannot be met; the strategy of trying to prove that even a Left-led Labour Party cannot deliver the goods, a strategy based upon internal manoeuvre. (*London Labour Briefing*, March 1984)

Such internal manoeuvring within the party can of course be of particular significance in situations where the local Labour party claims, or has achieved, some role in the Labour group's decision-making process. In such circumstances councillors may well feel obliged to confront, or to accommodate, critics within the party before making final decisions in group, in committee or in full council. This can lead to confusion and delays: as one officer put it – 'you can't get a decision because they're looking over their shoulder'. Such problems could become particularly awkward if a local party did indeed have the power to determine group, and thereby council, decisions for such a divorce between political power and legal responsibility seems a good recipe for periodic stalemate or conflict.

Problems of stalemate or paralysis may not only arise from council-union disputes or from factional or sectarian infighting. We have also seen in Chapter 3 the problems which can arise in trying to accommodate some of the left's 'new' issues alongside traditional Labour priorities. Even the relations between new issues may not be wholly trouble-free: at the GLC for example black dissatisfaction with the workings of the women's committee support unit led to an internal inquiry which finally concluded that the unit had been suffering not only from mismanagement but from institutional racism. The fact that amidst the turmoil the unit continued to serve and advise hundreds of women's groups throughout Greater London shows how commitment may overcome misfortune but the whole episode identified yet another possible source of mutual suspicion and division on the left.

Of course all political movements suffer from divisions from time to time but divisions on the left can have a rancour and an intensity of a particularly high order since they are often couched not, for example, in terms of better or worse judgement but of 'correctness' or 'mistakes' in ideology or of solidarity or betrayal. Everything is refracted through the ideological lens of socialism (however defined) and judged accordingly, thereby creating a private world, entrance to which is only available to those who have mastered the language and symbols of socialist discourse. This in turn contributes to another possible weakness of the new urban left namely that of estrangement from the day-to-day lives of ordinary citizens.

Estrangement

Kogan and Kogan (1983, p. 180) have written of the growth of 'institutional incest' among Labour councillors in recent years, citing the large number of them who are employed by councils or by council-funded voluntary organizations. In Camden for example 48 per cent of Labour councillors were dependent directly or indirectly on councils for their living, in Lewisham 55 per cent. Other commentators have identified a 'public service' class of Labour councillor dependent for their livelihood on local government, on councillors' allowances, on council-funded voluntary groups, or on public sector unions (Lipsey, 1982; Walker, 1983). In addition there have of course been the various appointments of political activists to positions within local authorities, whether to overtly political posts such as personal assistants to chairs, or to new jobs in newly-created units, or to established posts in the professional bureaucracy.

Of course the appointment of political sympathizers to positions of power or influence is not nowadays peculiar to the new urban left. Similar tactics in respect of the civil service and the health authorities for example have been adopted by the Thatcher government, though that in itself hardly constitutes a recommendation for the practice. The particular problem of concern here is that the combination of political appointments and 'public service' councillors does nothing to counterbalance, and probably aggravates, other tendencies in the private world of socialist activism towards estrangement from those outside. As Beresford and Croft (1982, pp. 5 and 7) observed, on the basis of their own experiences in Wandsworth:

> Where we live, for example, the interlocking of such organisations, like the Labour Party, community groups and paid professionals through the overlap of people between them, means that the exclusion of most local people, albeit that this is unintentional, is likely to be exacerbated . . . Instead, socialists mainly seem to talk to each other. Their whole organisation and ways of work collude to a kind of insularity among them. Their debates are largely internal.

Even when they are aware of the problem one common reaction among party activists is to try and link up with or build bridges to other activists, in community groups, in black organizations or in the women's movement for example. But in so far as such moves are successful they may lead to little more than cross membership: what they do not do is to bridge the gap between the various activists and the millions of people watching *Dallas*.

One result of this can be the problem identified by Deakin (1984, p. 23):

> Cross membership between local voluntary bodies and the local Party is common now in many inner city areas. The result is sometimes closer to farce than democracy: a stage army whose cast is in the final stages of meeting addiction engages in sham manoeuvres that are passed off as negotiation between the statutory and voluntary sectors.

The danger here is first that such patterns of activity can easily fuel suspicions that local socialism really is some form of private political machine doling out jobs and grants to those members who are in good ideological standing, and second that the whole syndrome of inter-locking organizations, internal debates, cross membership and meeting addiction adds to the estrangement of the left from the rest of the community. As Rustin (1984, p. 12) has pointed out the 'left-wing movement for the renewal of the [Labour] party since 1979 has . . . been seriously marred by somewhat simplistic and "vanguardist" ideas . . . [and] has over-estimated the representativeness of existing activists'. The outcome of this can be that activists 'see struggling for what *they* want as synonymous with struggling for what local working class people want' (Beresford and Croft, 1982, p. 6; emphasis in original).

A militantly proclaimed self-identification of the party and its activists with the people is of course one way of trying to cope with estrangement but it can take strange forms. Thus in 1982 Jessica Wanamaker, a Southwark Labour councillor representing a Bermondsey ward, assured Channel 4's *A Week in Politics* that 'the party does represent the local population to a very large extent, and I think there's no getting away from that', apparently oblivious of the fact that the party had sustained earlier in the year a substantial slump in its vote at the borough elections, a slump which moreover was to be maintained in council by-election defeats in 1983 and 1984. The previous year, after the left took control of the victorious GLC Labour group, *London Labour Briefing* (June 1981) proclaimed that 'London's Ours': this strangely proprietorial claim to the fruits of Londoners' voting decisions had distinct echoes of the now notorious wartime slogan that '*your* courage, *your* cheerfulness, *your* resolution' would 'bring *us* victory' (my emphasis).

This phenomenon of a somewhat proprietorial self-identification with the working class is of course encouraged by that sociological reductionism which Hindess has observed and which was referred to in Chapter 2, that is to say the left's belief that

> the interests of the working class are . . . inherent in the capitalist structure of the economy and they therefore exist quite independently of whether significant numbers of the working class are prepared to recognise them as such. (Hindess, 1983, p. 127)

Given this premise of course, socialist activists can see their own political aspirations as being 'objectively' the same as those of the workers for they 'know that the real working-class is out there somewhere, patiently awaiting the socialist call', and that there is a 'pre-given majority for socialism in British social structure just waiting to be realized' (Hindess, 1983, pp. 100 and 119). This sociological reductionism also helps to explain why it is that while constantly in danger of sliding into insularity and incestuousness the left simultaneously sets great store by campaigning and mobilizing in the community since in doing so it hopes to realize that supposedly pre-given majority for socialism.

However, as we have seen, this campaigning and mobilizing has heavily preceptoral overtones, with great stress on explaining the policies of Labour councils and building up support for socialist strategies. Thus one activist demanded that 'local public meetings with creche facilities should be held frequently *not only* to explain our radical policies but to *mobilise* people on the basis of them' (*London Labour Briefing*, February 1984, emphasis in original). But to explain is to talk, not to listen, to tell, not to ask, and to be mobilized is not the same as volunteering. The public are seen as a cross between an audience and a reserve army, not as actors in their own right who may have legitimately different opinions of their own. Indeed one of the very real problems of some left activists is their difficulty in conceiving that there can be legitimately different opinions to their own once everything has been explained. Only callous self-interest (in the case of capitalists and their fellow travellers), naive self-delusion (in the case of bourgeois reformers) and false consciousness (in the case of not-yet-socialist workers) are thought to stand in the way of the universal realization that objective reality coincides with the view from the socialist left: all else is mystification, to be dispelled by political education and campaigning by the party.

Preceptoral politics and party chauvinism are the logical outcomes of such an attitude and their implicit elitism does not sit easily with the idea of a local socialism whose aim is genuinely to devolve power to the people. The preceptoral elitism and the social incestuousness of left-wing activists could yet estrange local socialism from its potential constituency in much the same way as paternalism and introversion sometimes estranged municipal labourism from its constituency in earlier decades.

To have discussed local socialism in terms of such possibilities as estrangement from the people, disabling internal divisions and possible political defeat will no doubt be seen in some quarters as unduly critical and unduly pessimistic. None the less such possible outcomes cannot be dismissed out of hand and a recognition of pitfalls can help greatly in their avoidance. Moreover these particular problems are largely, though not wholly, problems of strategy and style and do not necessarily call into question the fundamental plausibility of a local road to socialism. There are however those who would do so and for whom the whole experience is misconceived: to them no amount of tackling the problems of strategy and style can overcome a basic flaw in local socialism.

Delusions

From a variety of standpoints some critics argue that local socialism simply cannot provide any kind of road to socialism since it is based on one or other of a number of delusions. For example those committed to the revolutionary or insurrectionary route to socialism continue to dismiss the hopes placed in Labour Party activity at any level. Instead they argue that

> the left should build now an independent socialist party . . . Those who enter the Labour Party hoping to win it to a socialist project go in vain, for the political distance that they expect the party to cover . . . is just too great. (Looker and Coates, 1983, pp. 278 and 281)

For critics such as these internal campaigns within the Labour Party, local socialism, single-issue politics, all such forms of activity are a futile distraction from the task of building a new genuinely socialist party.

Other critics, while far from dismissive of the Labour Party, nevertheless suggest that local socialism evades crucial issues of national-level politics especially in relation to the economy. Thus SERA's *Local Socialism* working group recognized that

> Advocates of local economic planning have been described as 'hobbit socialists' because of an alleged failure to link their proposals for local action to the national and international processes which would swamp any purely local activity. (Taylor, 1982, p. 5)

Such criticisms echo those that were levelled in retrospect at the War on Poverty in the United States in the 1960s when

> fostering an ideology and apparatus for local democracy as a response to urban poverty whose causes were beyond the control of the localities . . . severed the politics of poverty from the administration of wealth. (Friedland, 1982, p. 133)

John Benington identified a similar problem:

> It's possible to talk about building from below . . . but there's a complete limit to how far you can do that while the overall structure of society is controlled otherwise. We've got to demand

government intervention to gain control over the operations of
private capital ... Now those two things together make sense.
When I hear people talking about co-operatives and small local
initiatives and so on I can't believe in them unless you do the other.
If I only hear people talking about the big macro-stuff, I can't
believe in it because it's just more manipulation of the apparatus.
(Quoted in Exit Photography Group, 1982, p. 190)

The proponents of local socialism however are far from unaware of
the importance of national economic policy. Donnison (1983, p. 11)
for example recognizes that locally based initiatives 'do not offer us a
means of knitting our own way out of a world-wide economic crisis'.
But that of course is not meant to be one of their functions. Their
functions include generating new 'proposals for products or patterns
of production which meet social needs ... [rather than] rely on
centralized, secretive and professionalized planning to do this'
(Taylor, 1982, p. 8) and trying to "prefigure" the more democratic
forms of economic management we hope socialism will make
possible' (Clarke and Griffiths, 1982, p. 28). The aim, in addition to
responding to local economic problems, is to develop new locally-
based inputs into whatever form of national-level economic policy-
making may be adopted: the intention is not to ignore, or to replace,
but to supplement and sometimes to contest those initiatives or
imperatives generated at the centre.

There is however another dimension to this problem of the scope
and ambitions of local level politics in the context of socialism. The
issue is that which is raised by Saunders in his writings on the
specificity of local politics. He argues that

Local politics are essentially consumption politics and local
campaigns around issues of consumption cannot be easily
integrated into a nationally organised class based movement
centred on the politics of production ... local struggles over the
provision of day nurseries, the prevention of school closures or the
improvement of council housing repair services have their own
specificity and cannot be treated as part of a much grander class
struggle for socialism ... [though] much can be achieved.
(Saunders, 1984, p. 45)

From this perspective it is clear that local struggles 'cannot, therefore,
simply be taken under the wing of a socialist movement whose
primary concern lies in national questions of economic policy'
(Saunders, 1980b). However such a conclusion invites one to move
the debate on to the question of what precisely should now be the
'primary concern' of the socialist movement. It is in examining some
of the recent responses to this question that we may begin to see signs

of the relevance and potential of local socialism which could prevent it from being little more than just another brief idea.

A lasting impact?

Before taking up the questions of what might be socialism's primary concern and of how local socialism might relate to it, it will be as well to recognize that one way in which local socialism may have a more lasting impact than that of a passing brief idea is at the level of local government policy and practice.

A new agenda

It may be that ultimately a major impact of local socialism will prove to have been the addition of new elements to the agenda of local government, elements which may come to be adopted beyond the authorities where they first originated.

Decentralized service delivery, the encouragement of voluntary organizations and community groups, municipal enterprise, popular planning and workers' co-operatives, race policies and women's initiatives all extend the range of activities or policy options open to local authorities. As in the case of Birmingham's decision in 1984 to move towards decentralization, they may be adopted individually in response to particular local needs rather than as part and parcel of some total ideological package. In particular it is also possible that local socialism's general emphasis on trying to respond to the varied needs of multiple constituencies defined by locality, race, sex, age, issue-orientation, etc., may prove of great relevance to the requirements of a more plural and more fragmented society, even if, as we have seen, that same emphasis could pose certain problems in constructing a new majority for socialism.

Local socialism has also raised important questions about professionalism and bureaucracy in local government and about the ways in which local authorities operate both inside the town halls and in relation to the community outside. New styles of working and new modes of communication with both employees and local residents have created the possibility of more open and more accessible local authorities, though it has to be said that this cannot be achieved merely by replacing the bureaucracy and its professional ideology by the party and its political ideology.

In adition to its impact on the agenda of local government local socialism may also have an impact on the agenda of socialism and to this possibility we may now turn.

A new paradigm

It is certainly true, as Saunders suggested, that 'national questions of economic policy' and of 'the politics of production' have long been primary concerns among socialists. However it is also true that a number of writers have begun to argue that expressing that concern through an enthusiasm for state ownership and central planning has become less and less plausible, especially in the light of experiences in Russia and Eastern Europe. In his search for a 'feasible socialism', for example, Nove has argued the case for a system based largely on a mixture of state, social and co-operative property and combining a degree of planning at the macro-economic level with self-management at the micro-economic level and with a key role for the market mechanism to prevent abuse of monopoly power and to ensure consumer choice: as a general rule he expresses 'a preference for small scale, as a means of maximising participation and a sense of "belonging" ' (Nove, 1983, p. 227). Hodgson has argued the virtues of a similar approach to the problem of building a 'practical socialism' whose objective

> is to maximize autonomy while retaining coherence, to decentralize decision-making while retaining a measure of overall democratic control. It is a society in which both state and market exist but are subordinate to democracy. (Hodgson, 1984, p. 206)

Both Nove and Hodgson, and indeed others such as Tomlinson (1982), envisage a more variegated form of socialist economy than has conventionally been contemplated. Its components and their linkages would indeed provide a form of mixed economy – 'but in very different proportions from the present one' (Hodgson, 1984, p. 72). Amongst such components it is not difficult to envisage a place for some of the economic institutions of local socialism such as enterprise boards, popular planning and workers' co-operatives. Many of the new urban left would no doubt baulk at accepting the proposition that

> markets are a necessary component of any planned economy which aims at devolving decision-making power to the region, the locality, the community, and the workplace. (Hodgson, 1984, p. 185)

They tend to think rather in terms of meeting proven social needs, without specifying too clearly the mechanisms or the criteria by which various specific and possibly conflicting needs are to be regarded as unequivocally proven. None the less the general drift of the arguments of writers such as Nove and Hodgson is clearly towards the sort of decentralized and variegated socialist economy in which there would certainly be space for many of the ventures now being undertaken within local socialism.

Whatever their specific differences Nove, Hodgson and the new urban left share a general commitment to the notion that socialism entails a great measure of participation and self-government both in the economy and in other areas of life. This in turn raises other issues apart from those of institutional structure. In particular it invites us to confront the problem of the ability of people to play the part assigned to them in models of self-governing socialism. Hodgson recognizes the crucial importance of this problem and argues that questions of economic reform by central government must take second place and that

> extensions of democracy, participation, decentralization and autonomy should be pressed for first . . . Reforms from the centre should not distract us from the immediate tasks of extending participation and autonomy in our everyday lives. (Hodgson, 1984, pp. 209–10)

The importance here attached to extending popular experience of democratic practices echoes that found in Kitching's *Rethinking Socialism*. Kitching urges socialists to 'encourage any and all activities which involve *turning a passive citizenry into an active one* (even if they are active in ways . . . which are mutually contradictory) since without it the construction of *democratic* socialism is impossible'. Such a socialism, he recognizes, 'requires of workers both imagination and self-confidence' and would demand 'a citizenry of the greatest knowledge, sophistication and self-discipline'. Because of this 'the slow but determined self-construction of such a class is the primary socialist task within capitalism' (Kitching, 1983, pp. 14, 23, 44–5; emphases in original). Here, clearly, he foreshadows Hodgson's proposition that

> The participatory socialist society of the future has to be prefigured within the capitalism of the present. Without examples to point to, people will never be generally convinced of the validity of socialism. (Hodgson, 1984, p. 153)

The Hodgson/Nove formulation enabled us to see a role for local socialism in the economy of a decentralized self-governing socialism. So too the Hodgson/Kitching formulation suggests its role in the polity of such a socialism, namely that of contributing, through such policies as going local, popular planning and the encouragement of community groups, to the development of a citizenry with the confidence and the skills required to exercise democratic control over economic and social institutions.

It is of course far from surprising that elements of local socialism should find a place in the hypothetical prospectus of a self-governing socialism since, as we have seen in Chapter 2, its own emergence owed much to the desire to explore decentralist alternatives to Labour's traditional conception of socialism as a marriage between public corporations and parliamentary democracy. This does however beg the question of whether there are any reasons to expect the emergence of a decentralized, self-governing socialism within which the policies and practices of local socialism could play their part. To anticipate any such development is to argue that the accepted paradigms which have dominated British politics for the past four decades have been, or can be, effectively challenged by new ones.

Such however is the case argued by Marris on the basis of his analysis of British attempts to solve the social problems of the inner city during and since the 1960s. For Marris the failures of those attempts are important not only in themselves but also because they illustrate 'the disintegration of a concept of social policy which has prevailed in Britain for nearly forty years' (Marris, 1982, p. 71). He is therefore concerned to explain that disintegration and to seek a new concept of social policy.

He sees British policy in the 1960s and 1970s as exemplifying a liberal paradigm of social policy. This paradigm assumed first, that government was right to fight poverty and social inequity, and second that, armed with an understanding of economic and social processes, government had the power to use that knowledge for social purposes. The latter assumption, however, became questionable as government grew more dependent upon, and subservient to, an international economic system dominated by multi-nationals. The frustrations of urban policy thus reflected broader frustrations arising from government's inability to regulate the social consequences of the international economy. As the scale and concentration of economic organization in that economy grew to dwarf the power of any single government, so the liberal paradigm of social policy ceased to reflect reality. Moreover the sinking liberal paradigm dragged down with it a competing, socialist, paradigm, which while giving a special prominence to the role of class struggle, had also shared the liberal reliance on social scientific understanding and governmental power. In place of the liberal and socialist paradigms, with their assumption 'that government regulates economic activity in conformity with social ideals' there now emerged a new corporate paradigm which assumed 'that government must regulate social expectations in accordance with the requirements of the economy'. Government now became not 'a magisterial arbiter between economic and social needs . . . but an entrepreneur trying to make the most of its country's chances in a competitive international market' (Marris, 1982, pp. 102–3). Marris rejects the corporate paradigm and sees the best prospects for an alternative to be found in the convergence of a number of distinct movements and campaigns, including the environmental movement, the women's movement, assertions of racial identity and culture and community action and development. In their differing ways all these emphasize the need for a decentralized and democratic control of the economy and for economic management to be infused with a sense of social responsibility. This alternative paradigm is one which 'reintegrates government with the co-operative management of everyday life, as a pervasive, decentralized process of mutual accommodation' (Marris, 1982, pp. 106–7), and it would seem to have a clear resemblance to local socialism in many respects. At this point a sceptical reader might begin to wonder whether Marris has not fallen prey to a danger of which he himself warns, namely that with the disintegration of a dominant paradigm public policy may fall prey to impractical intellectual and ideological fads. The alternative paradigm may sound very attractive but how do we get there from here? Marris suggests that the journey requires the abandonment of a pre-occupation with the structural metaphor in terms of which urban and other social problems have come to be described. 'This structural metaphor was introduced from the Left . . . because it represented the inter-connections between neighbourhood, city, nation and the international economy as an indivisible set of relationships' (Marris, 1982, p. 111). The problem with the structural metaphor is its static quality, with all the elements locked together into immobility, offering no prospect of change or development. It ignores the relationships between the elements of the structure, relationships which are not fixed and inert like cement between bricks, but which must be continually renewed, or reproduced, in everyday life.

Whether these relationships are in fact reproduced depends on whether people continue to believe that they must conform to them. For much of the time people do so believe, but Marris suggests that under certain conditions a process of questioning may begin. When established patterns of reward and punishment, of opportunity and obligation, change or become confused then people may choose to behave differently: so may they also when new relationships are positively canvassed as an alternative to the old, as they are by the women's and anti-racist movements. By adopting the metaphor of relationships rather than of structure, some possibility of leverage is revealed, a possibility which might produce those changes necessary for the alternative paradigm to replace the corporate paradigm. If the alternative paradigm were to take hold 'a combination of community organization, trade union organization and local government could then begin to take back control of the land, skills, revenue, assets, pension funds it collectively owns to work out a co-operative plan for the social as well as economic future' (Marris, 1982, p. 127).

This may all seem headily optimistic to those for whom structural accounts are everything, and to whom a metaphor of relationships smacks of a naive voluntarism, yet it is clearly very much in tune with those notions of pre-figurative politics which have characterized much of local socialism.

Marris did not of course set out with the specific intention of providing some form of rationale for the policies and practices of local socialism. He does however suggest why a new paradigm of social policy may now be needed and also, by implication, how some of the elements of local socialism could play a part in the creation as well as in the operation of that new paradigm. More specifically, through his concern with the canvassing of new relationships, he enters on to territory similar to that explored by Hodgson and Kitching, for in their different ways all three point to the crucial importance for socialism – and especially for the development of a self-governing socialism – of the broadening and deepening of democratic practice amongst the citizenry.

Kitching (1983, p. 131) has written of the need 'to remarry socialist ideas with much older concepts of *civitas* . . . of the duties and powers as well as the passive "rights" of the citizen' and, as we have seen, he has identified the development of an active and responsible citizenry as the 'primary socialist task' of our time. In so far as local socialism proves able to contribute, through its emphases on decentralization, popular planning, local initiative, workers' co-operatives and voluntary and community groups, to the carrying out of that task then it may aspire to being something more than just a brief idea. In helping, through a wider democratic practice, to develop a new paradigm of social policy and of socialism it could make a considerable impact on contemporary and future politics. In order to do so however it would need to curb any tendencies towards party chauvinism or towards a preceptoral elitism of activists intent on mobilizing people into the 'correct' political position. Instead it should remember the wise words of Tony Benn:

Democracy can be properly described as the institutionalisation of a process by which society can learn from its own experience – and especially by its own mistakes. (Benn, 1980, p. 124)

As well as raising problems about the relations between people and party at the local level, local socialism also poses questions about the relations between the local and the national levels of government.

This is true for example of the question of how the problem of inequality is to be tackled. It has often been alleged that the price of securing equality would be the destruction of liberty and diversity: without conceding this, many socialists have certainly tended to see a centralized redistribution of resources as an essential element of socialist egalitarianism (Sharpe, 1982). Given the existing differential social geography of Britain a wholly decentralized political and economic system could enable wealthy areas such as South Kensington or Eastbourne to perpetuate their good fortune rather than contribute to poorer areas. Moreover, although Sidney Webb (1920, p. vii) defended local diversity because 'those who did not like the arrangements of Hampstead would always be able to move to Highgate', if such voting with the feet occurred on any large scale the geographical polarization of social classes and ethnic groups, and of mobile resources, could become even more marked than at present.

How could this be avoided? A national system of internal passports would clearly contradict the libertarian impulses behind decentralization. Should we conclude that nationally enforced territorial equality is therefore a pre-requisite of a decentralized socialism? And if we do, does local socialism become anything more than the handmaiden of state centralism? Such problems are not purely hypothetical. The disposition of resources is crucial to socialist economic policy, and local economic planning and local enterprise boards are often seen as an important element of local socialism. Yet at Labour's 1982 local government conference delegates were warned 'that such boards could not be given the freedom to act in ways which went against the national economic planning framework which Labour is promising as part of its alternative economic strategy' (*Labour Weekly*, 19 February 1982), a warning which suggested a rather low degree of attachment to ideas of local autonomy and a somewhat centralist attitude to problems of national–local relationships.

The latter are problems which the Labour Party has rarely considered in great detail and its occasional attempts to do so have not been notably successful (cf. Gyford and James, 1983). The main reason for this is of course that ever since it became one of the major parties of state Labour has seen socialism as something to be secured mainly by economic redistribution from above rather than by political empowerment from below. The emergence of local socialism, however, may now stimulate a challenge to that approach.

Of course the ability of people to respond effectively to political empowerment, if offered, may well relate to the availability of resources, both material and social, and it would therefore be foolish not to recognize that empowerment without redistribution might be something of a charade. Yet redistribution without empowerment, which has been the recipe thus far, seems likely to lead to little beyond the limited, though real, gains of the welfare state.

If there is to be a future beyond the welfare state, and if it is not to lie in the new right's mixture of economic liberalism and political authoritarianism, then the Labour Party will need to take the politics of empowerment more seriously than has been the case in the past. Doing so, of course, may well create certain problems of its own, for as Hindess (1983, p. 81) has pointed out:

> Once new democratic mechanisms have developed there can be no guarantee that socialists will approve of the decisions they generate ... Conflicts of this kind are an inevitable feature of a democratically organized society, and an extension of democratization must also extend the opportunities for them to occur.

There are some who will not be quite so amenable as Hindess to the prospect of un-socialist decisions emerging from an extended democracy. We saw, for example, at the end of the previous chapter, the possible conflict that could arise between a process of greater democratization and a strategy of socialist mobilization. It is an uneasy awareness of this problem which underlies what sometimes seems to be

> a profound ambiguity in the Left towards mass involvement in public life, an ambiguity which is rarely expressed publicly but which is a powerful determinant of much actual Left political activity. For, of course, if one's politics are based upon views which one knows not to be widely shared, one will necessarily view the extension and deepening of public life somewhat ambiguously. (Kitching, 1983, p. 17)

The politics of empowerment might therefore prove to be something of a Pandora's box for the left. However, if local socialism does turn out to have placed the subject on Labour's agenda, perhaps as the first step towards a new paradigm of socialist politics, then it may yet have consequences beyond the particular localities where it now operates.

References

Anderson, V. (1979), *The Liabilities of the Left*, a Clause 4 Pamphlet (Southampton: Clause 4 Publications).

Anderson, V. (1983), 'Liberal on the left', *Chartist*, May/June, p. 30.

Ashton, F. (1981), 'Local economic planning' in Labour Co-ordinating Committee, *Municipal Socialism: Its Past and Future Prospects* (Wandsworth: Wandsworth Community Publications), pp. 5–9.

Attlee, C. R. (n.d.), *Local Government and the Socialist Plan*, Socialist League Forum Lecture No. 7 (London: Socialist League).

Baine, S. (1975), *Community Action and Local Government*, Occasional Papers on Social Administration No. 59, London School of Economics.

Barker, Sir E. (1963), *Political Thought in England 1848 to 1914* (London: OUP).

Bell, D. S. and Criddle, B. (1984), *The French Socialist Party* (London: OUP).

Benington, J. (1981), 'Knowing better: Acting more effectively' in *Local Enterprise and Workers Plans*, Institute for Workers' Control Pamphlet 79 (Nottingham: Institute for Workers' Control), pp. 15–18.

Benn, A. (1980), *Arguments for Socialism* (Harmondsworth: Penguin).

Benn, A. (1981), *Arguments for Democracy* (London: Cape).

Benn, A. (1983), 'From defeat to victory', *New Socialist*, September/October, pp. 32–5.

Beresford, P. and Croft, S. (1982), *A Future for Socialism?* (Battersea: Battersea Community Action).

Beresford, P. and Croft, S. (1983), 'Making our own plans', *Chartist*, no. 94, pp. 26–7.

Beresford, P. and Croft, S. (1984), 'Welfare pluralism: the new face of Fabianism', *Critical Social Policy*, no. 9, pp. 19–39.

Berger, P. (1977), *Pyramids of Sacrifice* (Harmondsworth: Penguin).

Bevan, A. (1952), *In Place of Fear* (London: Heinemann).

Bingham, V. (1981), 'Community politics', *New Outlook*, vol. 21, no. 1, pp. 22–3.

Blackmore, R. D. (1982), 'Community politics: its history and purpose', *New Outlook*, vol. 24, no. 1, pp. 16–19.

Blazyca, G. (1983), *Planning is Good for You: The Case for Popular Control* (London: Pluto Press).

Blunkett, D. (1981a), 'Struggle for democracy', *New Socialist*, September/October, p. 33.

Blunkett, D. (1981b), 'Towards a socialist social policy', *Local Government Policy Making*, vol. 8, no. 1, pp. 95–103.

Blunkett, D. (1982), 'Sheffield steel', *New Socialist*, November/December, pp. 56–7.

Blunkett, D. (1984), Interview in M. Boddy and C. Fudge (eds), *Local Socialism?*(London: Macmillan), pp. 242–60.

Blunkett, D. and Green, G. (1984), *Building from the Bottom*, Fabian Tract 491 (London: Fabian Society).

Boaden, N. (1971), *Urban Policy-Making*(Cambridge: CUP).

Boaden, N., Goldsmith, M., Hampton, W. and Stringer, P. (1982), *Public Participation in Local Services* (London: Longman).

Boddy, M. and Fudge, C. (eds) (1984), *Local Socialism?* (London: Macmillan).

Branson, N. (1975), *Britain in the Nineteen Twenties* (London: Weidenfeld & Nicolson).

Branson, N. (1979), *Poplarism 1919–25* (London: Lawrence & Wishart).

Branson, N. and Heinemann, M. (1971), *Britain in the Nineteen Thirties* (London: Weidenfeld & Nicolson).

Brown, B. E. (1982), *Socialism of a Different Kind* (Westport, Conn.: Greenwood Press).

Butler, D. and Kavanagh, D. (1980), *The British General Election of 1979* (London: Macmillan).

Bye, B. and Beattie, J. (1982), *Local Economic Planning and the Unions* (London: Workers' Educational Association).

Calder, R. (1941), *Start Planning Britain Now*(London: Kegan Paul).

Canovan, M. (1981), *Populism* (London: Junction Books).

Capital and Class (1982), 'A socialist GLC in a capitalist Britain?', no. 18, pp. 117–33.

Carvel, R. (1984), *Citizen Ken* (London: Chatto & Windus).

Cawson, A. and Saunders, P. (1983), 'Corporatism, competitive politics and class struggle', in R. King (ed.), *Capital and Politics* (London: Routledge), pp. 8–27.

Clarke, C. and Griffiths, D. (1982), *Labour and Mass Politics* (London: Labour Co-ordinating Committee).

Clarke, R. (1983), 'GLC Women's Committee at the crossroads', *London Labour Briefing*, May, pp. 14–15.

Coates, K. (1976), *The New Workers Co-operatives* (Nottingham: Spokesman Books).

Cockburn, C. (1977), *The Local State* (London: Pluto Press).

Cole, G. D. H. (1948), *A Short History of the British Working Class Movement 1789–1947*(London: Allen & Unwin).

Corrigan, P. (1979), 'The local state: the struggle for democracy', *Marxism Today*, July, pp. 203–9.

Coventry, Liverpool, Newcastle and North Tyneside Trades Councils (1980), *State Intervention in Industry: a worker's inquiry* (Newcastle: Coventry, Liverpool, Newcastle and North Tyneside Trades Councils).

Croft, S. and Beresford, P. (1984), 'Poor politics', *New Socialist*, October, pp. 57–9.

Crossman, R. (1977), *The Diaries of a Cabinet Minister*, vol. 3 (London: Hamish Hamilton/Cape).

David, J. (1983), 'Walsall and decentralisation', *Critical Social Policy*, no. 7, pp. 75–9.

Deakin, N. (1984), 'Two cheers for decentralisation', in A. Wright, J. Stewart and N. Deakin, *Socialism and Decentralisation*, Fabian Tract 496 (London: Fabian Society).

Donnison, D. (1983), *Urban Policies: a new approach*, Fabian Tract 487 (London: Fabian Society).

Donoughue, B. and Jones, G. W. (1973), *Herbert Morrison: Portrait of a Politician* (London: Weidenfeld & Nicolson).

Drucker, H. M. (1979), *Doctrine and Ethos in the Labour Party* (London: Allen & Unwin).

Duncan, G. (1983), 'Australia: The ALP, socialism and reform', in P. Davis (ed.), *Social Democracy in the Pacific* (Auckland: Ross), pp. 9–27.

Dunleavy, P. (1979), *Urban Political Analysis* (London: Macmillan).

Dunleavy, P. (1980), 'The political implications of sectoral cleavages and the growth of state employment', *Political Studies*, vol. xxviii, nos. 3 and 4, pp. 364–83 and 527–49.

Dunleavy, P. (1981), *The Politics of Mass Housing in Britain, 1945–1975* (London: OUP).

Dunlop, P. (1984), 'Liverpool council and class politics', in *Liverpool Fights the Tories* (London: Militant), pp. 8–9.

Dunn, J. (1984), *The Politics of Socialism* (Cambridge: CUP).

Elcock, H. (1981), 'Tradition and change in Labour Party politics: The decline and fall of the city boss', *Political Studies*, vol. xxix, no. 3, pp. 439–47.

Evans, A. (1973), *Economics of Residential Location* (London: Macmillan).

Exit Photography Group (1982), *Survival Programmes in Britain's Inner Cities* (Milton Keynes: Open University Press).

Fitzwalter, R. and Taylor, D. (1981), *Web of Corruption* (London: Granada).

Foot, M. (1975), *Aneurin Bevan: 1897–1945* (London: Paladin).

Foot, M. (1984), *Another Heart and Other Pulses* (London: Collins).

Forsyth, M. (1981), *Re-servicing Britain* (London: Adam Smith Institute).

Fraser, D. (1979), *Power and Authority in the Victorian City* (Oxford: Blackwell).

Friedland, R. (1982), *Power and Crisis in the City* (London: Macmillan).

Garton-Ash, T. (1983), *The Polish Revolution* (London: Cape).

Gladstone, F. (1979), *Voluntary Action in a Changing World* (London: Bedford Square Press).

Glassberg, A. D. (1981), *Representation and Urban Community* (London: Macmillan).

GLC (1983a), *GLC Women's Committee: Working for Women in London* (London: GLC).

GLC (1983b), *Jobs for a Change* (London: GLC Economic Policy Group).

GLC (1984), *Challenge Racism!* (London: GLC).

GLEB (1984), *A Strategy for Co-operation* (London: GLEB).

Gordon, I. and Whiteley, P. (1979), 'Social class and political attitudes: the case of Labour councillors', *Political Studies*, vol. xxvii, no. 1, pp. 99–113.

Goss, S. (1984), 'Women's initiatives in local government' in M. Boddy and C. Fudge (eds), *Local Socialism?* (London: Macmillan), pp. 109–32.

Greaves, B. (1980), 'The future of community politics', *New Outlook*, vol. 20, no. 2, pp. 14–18.

Green, D. G. (1981), *Power and Party in an English City* (London: Allen & Unwin).

Grosskurth, A. (1985), 'Bringing back the Braddocks', *Roof*, January/February, pp. 19–23.

Gustafson, B. (1976), *Social Change and Party Reorganization: The New Zealand Labour Party Since 1945* (London: Sage).

Gyford, J. and James, M. (1983), *National Parties and Local Politics* (London: Allen & Unwin).

Hadley, R. and Hatch, S. (1981), *Social Welfare and the Failure of the State* (London: Allen & Unwin).

Hain, P. (1980a), *Neighbourhood Participation* (London: Temple Smith).

Hain, P. (1980b), *On Reviving the Labour Party*, Institute for Workers' Control Pamphlet 71 (Nottingham: Institute for Workers' Control).

Hain, P. (ed.) (1980c), *The Crisis and the Future of the Left* (London: Pluto Press).

Hain, P. (1983), *The Democratic Alternative* (Harmondsworth: Penguin).

Hain, P. and Hebditch, S. (1978), *Radicals and Socialism*, Institute for Workers' Control Pamphlet 58 (Nottingham: Institute for Workers' Control).

Hall, S. *et al.* (1969), 'May Day Manifesto' in C. Oglesby (ed.), *The New Left Reader* (New York: Grove Press), pp. 111–43.

Hanby, V. (1974), 'A changing Labour elite: the National Executive of the Labour Party, 1900–1972' in I. Crewe (ed.), *British Political Sociology Yearbook*, vol. 1 (London: Croom Helm), pp. 126–58.

Harrington, I. (1971), 'Young turks of the town halls', *New Statesman*, 16 July.

Harrison, P. (1983), *Inside the Inner City* (Harmondsworth: Penguin).

Hatfield, M. (1978), *The House the Left Built* (London: Gollancz).

Hatton, D. (1984), 'Fight for Labour landslide', in *Liverpool Fights the Tories* (London: Militant), p. 7.

Heilbroner, R. (1972), 'Roots of the socialist dilemma', *Dissent*, Summer, pp. 463–70.

Higgins, J., Deakin, N., Edwards, J. and Wicks, M. (1983), *Government and Urban Poverty* (London: Blackwell).

Hill, M. J. (1972), *The Sociology of Public Administration* (London: Weidenfeld and Nicolson).

Hindess, B. (1971), *The Decline of Working Class Politics* (London: Granada).

Hindess, B. (1983), *Parliamentary Democracy and Socialist Politics* (London: Routledge & Kegan Paul).

Hobsbawm, E. (1981), *'The Forward March of Labour Halted?'* (London: Verso).

Hobsbawm, E. (1982), 'The state of the left in Western Europe', *Marxism Today*, October, pp. 8–15.

Hobsbawm, E. (1983), 'Labour's lost millions', *Marxism Today*, October, pp. 7–13.

Hodgson, G. (1984), *The Democratic Economy* (Harmondsworth: Penguin).

Horvat, B., Markovic, M. and Supek, R. (eds) (1975), *Self-Governing Socialism: A Reader* (White Plains, N.Y.: International Arts and Sciences Press).

Jeffers, J. (1980), *The Future of Municipal Socialism in Wandsworth* (Wandsworth: Wandsworth Community Publications).

Johnson, R. W. (1973), 'The British political elite, 1955–1972', *European Journal of Sociology*, vol. 14, no. 1, pp. 35–77.

Kaplan, J. (1975), *Lincoln Steffens* (London: Cape).

Kitching, G. (1983), *Rethinking Socialism* (London: Methuen).

Kogan, M. and Kogan, D. (1983), *The Battle for the Labour Party*, 2nd edn (London: Fontana).

Kolakowski, L. (1977), 'Introduction', in L. Kolakowski and S. Hampshire (eds.), *The Socialist Idea: A Reappraisal* (London: Quartet Books), pp. 1–17.

Kraushaar, R. (1979), 'Pragmatic radicalism', *International Journal of Urban and Regional Research*, vol. 3, pp. 61–80.

Kraushaar, R. (1981), 'Policy without protest: the dilemma of organising for change in Britain', in M. Harloe (ed.), *New Perspectives in Urban Change and Conflict* (London: Heinemann), pp. 101–21.

Labour Co-ordinating Committee (1981), *Can Local Government Survive?* (London: Labour Co-ordinating Committee).

Labour Co-ordinating Committee (1982), *The Realignment of the Right* (London: Labour Co-ordinating Committee).

Labour Co-ordinating Committee (1984), *Go Local to Survive: Decentralisation in Local Government* (London: Labour Co-ordinating Committee).

Lapping, A. (ed.) (1970), *Community Action*, Fabian Tract 400 (London: Fabian Society).

Lawrence, R. (1983), 'Voluntary action: a stalking house for the right?', *Critical Social Policy*, vol. 2, no. 3, pp. 14–30.

Leeson, P. (1981), 'Capitalism, statism and socialism' in M. Prior (ed.), *The Popular and the Political* (London: Routledge), pp. 1–19.

Leys, S. (1978), *Chinese Shadows* (Harmondsworth: Penguin).

Lifton, R. J. (1967), *Thought Reform and the Psychology of Totalism* (Harmondsworth: Penguin).

Lindblom, C. (1977), *Politics and Markets* (New York: Basic Books).

Lineberry, R. L. and Sharkansky, I. (1978), *Urban Politics and Public Policy* (New York: Harper & Row).

Lipset, S. M. and Raab, C. (1979), *The Politics of Un-reason* (London: Heinemann).

Lipsey, D. (1982), 'Labour's new (non-manual) breed of councillor', *Sunday Times*, 19 September.

Livingstone, K. (1981), Interview in *Marxism Today*, November, pp. 16–20.

Livingstone, K. (1982), Report of speech to the Chartered Institute of Public Finance and Accountancy, *Public Finance and Accountancy*, September, pp. 34–7.

Livingstone, K. (1984), Interview in M. Boddy and C. Fudge (eds), *Local Socialism?* (London: Macmillan), pp. 260–83.

Loew, S. (1980), *An experiment in local democracy in France* Occasional Paper 1/80, Department of Town Planning, Polytechnic of the South Bank, London.

Loney, M. (1981), 'The British Community Development Projects: questioning the state', *Community Development Journal*, vol. 16, no. 11, pp. 55–66.

Loney, M. (1983), *Community Against Government* (London: Heinemann).

Looker, R. and Coates, D. (1983), 'Basic problems of socialist strategy', in D. Coates and G. Johnston (eds), *Socialist Strategies* (Oxford: Martin Robertson), pp. 241–82.

Markovic, M. (1982), *Democratic Socialism: Theory and Practice* (Brighton: Harvester Press).

Marris, P. (1982), *Community Planning and Conceptions of Change* (London: Routledge & Kegan Paul).

Marshall, Lord (1978), *The Marshall Inquiry on Greater London* (London: GLC).

Marwick, A. (1967), *The Deluge: British Society and the First World War* (Harmondsworth: Penguin).

Massey, D., Segal, L., Wainwright, H. (1984), 'Stop the great male moving right show!', *New Socialist*, January/February, pp. 18–22.

Mayo, M. (1979), 'Radical politics and community action', in M. Loney and M. Allen (eds), *The Crisis of the Inner City* (London: Macmillan).

McDonnell, K. (1983), 'Decentralisation: progress in London', *Local Socialism*, January/February, pp. 4–5.

McHenry, D. E. (1938), *The Labour Party in Transition 1931–1938* (London: Routledge).

Meacher, M. (1979), *Socialism with a Human Face* (London: Allen & Unwin).

Meadowcroft, M. (1982a), *Liberalism and the Left* (London: Liberator Publications).

Meadowcroft, M. (1982b), 'Papal parties?', a paper for the Liberalism and the Left conference, London, 4–5 December 1983.

Meadowcroft, M. (1984), 'The New (Liberal) Left', *Marxism Today*, February, pp. 14–18.

Merton, R. K. (1968), *Social Theory and Social Structure* (New York: Free Press).

Miliband, R. (1969), *The State in Capitalist Society* (London: Weidenfeld & Nicolson).

Militant (1984), *Liverpool Fights the Tories* (London: Militant).

Mole, S. (1980), 'Community politics revisited', *New Outlook*, vol. 20, nos. 6/7, pp. 13–19.

Mole, S. (1983), 'The Liberal Party and community politics', in V. Bogdanor (ed.), *Liberal Party Politics* (London: OUP), pp. 258–73.

Mulhearn, T. (1984), 'Twenty years of struggle', in *Liverpool Fights the Tories* (London: Militant), p. 10.

Nicholas, D. (1981), *Neighbourhood Offices: the Walsall Experience* (Wandsworth: Wandsworth Community Publications).

Nove, A. (1983), *The Economics of Feasible Socialism* (London: Allen & Unwin).

O'Malley, J. (1977), *The Politics of Community Action* (Nottingham: Spokesman Books).

Ouseley, H. (1984), 'Local authority race initiatives', in M. Boddy and C. Fudge (1984) (eds), *Local Socialism?* (London: Macmillan), pp. 133–59.

Paterson, W. and Thomas, A. (eds) (1977), *Social Democratic Parties in Western Europe* (London: Croom Helm).

Pimlott, B. (1980), 'The Labour Left', in C. Cook and I. Taylor (eds), *The Labour Party* (London: Longman), pp. 163–88.

122   The Politics of Local Socialism

Polsby, N. (1979), 'Introduction', in L. J. Sharpe (ed.), *Decentralist Trends in Western Democracy* (London: Sage), pp. 1–7.

Prior, M. and Purdy, D. (1979), *Out of the Ghetto* (Nottingham: Spokesman Books).

PSI (1983), *Police and People in London* (London: Policy Studies Institute).

Radice, G. (1979), *Community Socialism*, Fabian Tract 464 (London: Fabian Society).

Raine, J. W. and Webster, B. (1984), *Strategy, Choice and Support: A review of grant aid to voluntary and community organisations from the London Borough of Camden* (Birmingham: University of Birmingham, Institute of Local Government Studies).

Robinson, W. (1948), 'Labour and Local Government', in H. Tracey (ed.), *The British Labour Party* (London: Caxton), vol. II, pp. 177–90.

Roelofs, S. (1983), 'GLC Women's Committee – femocratism or feminism?', *London Labour Briefing*, April, pp. 18–20.

Rowbotham, S., Segal, L. and Wainwright, H. (1979), *Beyond the Fragments* (London: Merlin Press).

Rustin, M. (1983), 'Power to the provinces!', *Marxism Today*, January, pp. 24–31.

Rustin, M. (1984), 'Opening to the future', *New Socialist*, October, pp. 11–16.

Saunders, P. (1980a), *Urban Politics* (Harmondsworth: Penguin).

Saunders, P. (1980b), 'Local government and the state', *New Society*, 13 March.

Saunders, P. (1981), *Social Theory and the Urban Question* (London: Hutchinson).

Saunders, P. (1982), 'Why study central–local relations?', *Local Government Studies*, vol. 8, no. 2, pp. 55–66.

Saunders, P. (1984), 'Rethinking local politics', in M. Boddy and C. Fudge (eds), *Local Socialism?* (London: Macmillan), pp. 22–48.

Scraton, P. (1982), 'Policing and institutionalised racism on Merseyside', in D. Cowell, T. Jones and J. Young (eds), *Policing the Riots* (London: Junction Books), pp. 21–38.

Seabrook, J. (1978), *What Went Wrong?* (London: Victor Gollancz).

Seabrook, J. (1984), *The Idea of Neighbourhood* (London: Pluto Press).

Selucky, R. (1979), *Marxism, Socialism, Freedom* (London: Macmillan).

Shannon, J. B. (1940), 'County consolidation', *Annals of the American Academy of Political and Social Sciences*, vol. 207, pp. 168–75.

Sharman, N. (1981), 'Community work and the local economy: the influence of the British Community Development Projects', *Community Development Journal*, vol. 16, no. 2, pp. 142–7.

Sharpe, L. J. (1982), 'The Labour Party and the geography of inequality: a puzzle', in D. Kavanagh (ed.), *The Politics of the Labour Party* (London: Allen & Unwin), pp. 135–70.

Sharpe, L. J. and Newton, K. (1984), *Does Politics Matter?* (London: OUP).

Sik, O. (1976), *The Third Way* (London: Wildwood House).

Silburn, R. and Coates, K. (1970), *Poverty: the Forgotten Englishman* (Harmondsworth: Penguin).

Simey, M. (1982), 'Police authorities and accountability: The Merseyside

Experience', in D. Cowell, T. Jones and J. Young (eds), *Policing the Riots* (London: Junction Books), pp. 52–7.

Skinner, D. and Langdon, J. (1974), *The Story of Clay Cross* (Nottingham: Spokesman Books).

Smith, T. D. (1970), *An Autobiography* (Newcastle: Oriel Press).

Stevenson, J. (1984), *British Society, 1914–45* (Harmondsworth: Penguin).

Taylor, A. (1980), *Democratic Planning through Workers' Control* (London: Socialist Environment and Resources Association).

Taylor, A. (1982), *Council Action for a Socialist Economy* (London: Socialist Environment and Resources Association).

Thompson, E. P. (1974), 'An Open Letter to Leszek Kolakowski', in R. Miliband and J. Saville (eds), *The Socialist Register 1973* (London: Merlin Press), pp. 1–100.

Thompson, P. (1984), 'Liverpool Council rules O.K.?' Local Socialism, July, p. 1.

Tomlinson, J. (1982), *The Unequal Struggle?* (London: Methuen).

Vowles, J. (1983), 'New Zealand: social democracy in the balance', in P. Davis (ed.), *Social Democracy in the Pacific* (Auckland: Ross), pp. 28–47.

Wainwright, H. (1983), 'Popular planning: jobs for a change', *Chartist*, February/April, pp. 10–11.

Wainwright, H. (1984), 'The GLC: so what's new?', *Bulletin of the Socialist Society*, Autumn.

Walker, D. (1983), 'Local interest and representation: the case of "class" interest among Labour representation in inner London', *Government and Policy*, vol. 1, pp. 341–6.

Ward, C. (1978), 'Self-help socialism', *New Society*, 20 April.

Ward, M. (1981), *Job Creation by the Council*, Institute for Workers' Control Pamphlet 78 (Nottingham: Institute for Workers' Control).

Webb, S. (1910), 'Social movements' in A. W. Ward, G. W. Prothero and S. Leathes (eds), *The Cambridge Modern History* (Cambridge: CUP), Vol. XII, pp. 730–65.

Webb, S. (1917), *When Peace Comes*, Fabian Tract 181 (London: Fabian Society).

Webb, S. (1920), 'Introduction', in G. B. Shaw (ed.), *Fabian Essays in Socialism*, 1920 edn (London: Allen & Unwin and the Fabian Society), pp. i–xv.

Wells, H. G. (1959), 'A paper on administrative areas read before the Fabian Society', reprinted as an appendix in A. Maas (ed.), *Area and Power* (Glencoe, Ill.: The Free Press), pp. 206–21.

Whiteley, P. (1982), 'The decline of Labour's local party membership and electoral base, 1945–79', in D. Kavanagh (ed.), *The Politics of the Labour Party* (London: Allen & Unwin), pp. 111–34.

Whiteley, P. (1983), *The Labour Party in Crisis* (London: Methuen).

Wilding, P. (1981), *Socialism and Professionalism*, Fabian Tract 473 (London: Fabian Society).

Wilson, H. (1973), *Democracy in Local Affairs* (London: Labour Party).

Wolinetz, S. B. (1977), 'The Dutch Labour Party: a social democratic party in transition', in W. E. Paterson and A. H. Thomas (eds), *Social Democratic Parties in Western Europe* (London: Croom Helm), pp. 342–88.

Wolmar, C. (1984), 'Divided we stand', *New Socialist*, December, pp. 13–15.
Worpole, K. (1981), 'Volunteers for socialism', *New Society*, 29 January.
Wright, A. (1984), 'Decentralisation and the socialist tradition', in A. Wright, J. Stewart and N. Deakin, *Socialism and Decentralisation*, Fabian Tract 496 (London: Fabian Society), pp. 1–7.
Wright, A., Stewart, J. and Deakin, N. (1984), *Socialism and Decentralisation*, Fabian Tract 496 (London: Fabian Society).

Index